STEP-BY-STEP

PASTA

COOKBOOK

EDITED BY SUSAN TOMNAY

CRESCENT BOOKS
NEW YORK

CONTE

Green Olive and Eggplant Toss, page 27.

Minestrone with Pesto, page 32.

Gnocchi with Tomato Sauce, page 53.

Farfalle with Tuna, Mushrooms and Cream, page 73.

Semolina Gnocchi, page 110.

Baked Spaghetti Frittata, page 88.

The Publisher thanks the following for their assistance in the photography for this book:

Waterford Wedgwood;
Zyliss Australia;
Emile-Henry;
Antico's Fruitworld;
Nicholas;
Le Creuset.

Classic Lasagna, page 102.

Step-by-Step

When we test our recipes we rate them for ease of preparation.

A single symbol indicates a recipe that is simple and generally quick to make—perfect for beginners.

Two symbols indicate the need for just a little more care and a little more time.

Three symbols indicate special dishes that need more investment in time, care and patience—but the results are worth it.

Front cover: Farfalle Salad with Sun-dried Tomatoes and Spinach, page 24.
Inside front cover: Spaghetti and Mussels in Tomato and Herb Sauce (top) and Pasta Marinara, page 44.
Inside back cover: Linguine with Red Pepper Sauce (top) and Spirals with Green Sauce, page 20.

Pasta and Cheese

Pasta can be as simple or as extravagant as you like—depending
upon its accompanying sauce. Most pasta dishes are enhanced
by the addition of cheese. Pasta, cheese and salad makes a
well-balanced and delicious meal.

HOW TO COOK PASTA

Use a very large pan of water. For 1 lb of pasta you will need at least 16 cups of water. Bring water, salted if desired, to a rapid boil and add pasta gradually so that the water continues to boil. The pasta should be able to move freely to prevent it sticking together. Stir once with a long-handled fork or spoon to prevent pasta sticking to bottom of the pan.

Long pasta such as spaghetti should be eased into the water rather than broken. Hold one end and put the other end in the boiling water. As pasta softens, gently lower it into the water until it is all immersed. Make sure the water boils rapidly while pasta is cooking. Do not cover pan.

Some people like to add a few drops of olive oil to the water to help prevent sticking.

Timing of pasta cooking is very important. Follow the directions on the packet and before stated time is up, remove a piece and test it. It should still be firm (al dente). Dried pasta usually takes 8–12 minutes and fresh pasta about 3–6 minutes, depending on the size and thickness. Drain pasta into a colander as soon as it is ready.

Pasta is best used as soon as it is cooked but if you have to keep it warm for a while, drain and toss with a little olive oil to keep pieces separate. If it is to be used cold in a salad

Hold one end of long pasta and ease it into boiling water as it softens.

rinse thoroughly under cold water after cooking. Drain and toss in a little oil. Refrigerate.

The recipes in this book use dried pasta unless fresh pasta is specified. If you prefer, you can substitute fresh. Vary the cooking time accordingly.

Amount of pasta per person: For an average serving you will need $2^1/_2$–4 oz of dried pasta per person and 4–6 oz of fresh.

Use a vegetable peeler to shave fresh Parmesan for garnishes and salads.

To serve: The traditional way of serving pasta such as spaghetti or fettuccine is to divide cooked pasta into individual serving bowls and toss with a little of the sauce. The remaining sauce is then placed in a bowl at the table so guests can help themselves.

An easy way to serve is to return drained, cooked pasta to pan. Add sauce; toss until combined. Transfer to large serving bowl or divide between individual serving dishes.

LONG PASTA

There is an enormous variety of widths, thicknesses and shapes of long pasta. Round ones include spaghetti, vermicelli and spaghettini. Some, such as bucatini, have a hole through the middle to allow thin sauces to flow through.

Spaghetti is often served simply with oil and garlic. However, it can be served with any sauce which clings to

the pasta. Vermicelli can be used in the same way.

Flat, long pasta such as fettuccine, tagliatelle and linguine are also best with sauces which cling when strands are picked up.

Seafood, including mussels, is often served with long pasta but big, chunky pieces of vegetables and meat aren't easy to eat with any of the long pasta. Bolognese sauce goes well with spaghetti and tagliatelle.

To eat: Use a fork to spear a few strands and place the tip of the fork against a spoon. Twirl fork so strands wind around the fork. Or just push the fork against the plate and twirl.

SHORT PASTA

These are straight or shaped and sometimes tubular. Tubular and shaped short pasta retain the accompanying sauce well and are easy to pick up with most sauces, including chunky meat and vegetables. All short pastas are interchangeable.

CONCHIGLIE: Shell-shaped pasta which comes in various sizes. Large shells are excellent for baking with fillings such as seafood whereas small shells can be used in casseroles and soups or can be served cold in salads.

FARFALLE: Butterfly- or bow tie-shaped pasta. Excellent with meat or vegetable sauces.

FUSILLI: Twist or spiral pasta—good in salads and with meat sauces as the meat gets caught in the spirals.

MACARONI: Straight or curved (elbows) short lengths of pasta with a hole through the center. Often used in baked dishes.

PENNE: Straight short lengths with a smooth or ridged surface, with a wide hole through the middle. Ends are cut at an angle. Retain sauce well.

LASAGNA SHEETS: Flat or ridged sheets of pasta. Layered with sauces and then baked. Some need pre-cooking before layering. Follow the manufacturer's instructions.

FILLED PASTA

CANNELLONI TUBES: Pasta which have a hole big enough for filling with meat and vegetable sauces. After filling, they are baked with a sauce poured over the top to keep them moist.

RAVIOLI AND TORTELLINI: Pasta shapes with a variety of fillings including vegetable, chicken and meat. Buy them fresh or dried or make your own. They are cooked separately and usually served with mild sauces that don't overwhelm the flavor of the filling.

GNOCCHI

Small savory dumplings made with vegetables or semolina. They are poached and served with sauces.

PASTA FOR SOUPS

Many different shapes are available for adding to soups and casseroles. There are little stars (stelline), small versions of shells (conchiglie) and farfalle (butterflies or bow ties) and even pasta in the shape of letters of the alphabet.

CHEESE

Cheese, most commonly Parmesan, is often used in pasta dishes. Sometimes it is part of the sauce, sometimes simply used as a garnish.

For storage, it is preferable that hard cheeses be wrapped tightly in foil or kitchen paper and refrigerated. If you prefer to use plastic wrap, squeeze out as much air as possible and then wrap in foil as well.

Cheese used in pasta dishes should be freshly grated—avoid ready-grated cheeses.

Soft cheeses such as ricotta are excellent in stuffings because they help bind other ingredients together and have a pleasant texture. Refrigerate in a covered container.

PARMESAN is a hard granular, light yellow cheese with a very strong flavor which blends extremely well with meat, tomato and vegetable sauces as well as some creamy sauces and soups. It is not generally used with mushroom sauces or seafood. Parmesan cheese keeps for months if wrapped tightly before refrigeration.

Parmigiano-reggiano is the best type of Parmesan with a good strong flavor. It is available at most delicatessens. The rind should have its name marked on it. If you can't get it, try *Grana*. If you can't find either of these, use block Parmesan available from the dairy section of most supermarkets. Avoid ready-grated Parmesan.

GRUYÈRE is a form of firm Swiss cheese, pale yellow in color. Gruyère varies from dry and strong-flavored to a more mild creamy style. The creamy one is preferable in most sauces. Gruyère is an excellent melting cheese which draws hardly any threads. You can use a cheddar as a substitute if you prefer.

ROMANO is a hard granular cheese with a biting flavor. It has small holes throughout and is golden yellow, darkening with maturity. Sometimes it is used as a substitute for Parmesan cheese. Like Parmesan, it is often finely grated or shaved for use as a garnish to enhance the flavor of pasta dishes.

PECORINO is a hard granular cheese, pale yellow, darkening with maturity. It has a stronger, more piquant, tangy taste than Parmesan and can be used as a substitute for Parmesan if you enjoy the biting flavor. Like Parmesan, it stores for a long time.

RICOTTA is a moist, fine, white cheese with a sweet, delicate flavor. The texture is quite creamy. It is very good for use in the fillings for pasta dishes such as cannelloni and is quite often used in the cooking of sweet dishes.

BOCCONCINI AND OVOLINI are soft, moist, mild, almost white cheeses. Ovolini is a small version of bocconcini. If bought unpackaged from delicatessens, refrigerate in the whey that they come in and use within 3 days. Those sold in sealed bags have a use-by date on them—use within 3 days of opening.

MOZZARELLA is a soft, smooth cheese, pale yellow in color. It has a mild, sweet flavor and is excellent for recipes that have the cheese melted on top and for use in salads.

GORGONZOLA is a soft, creamy, blue-veined cheese with quite a pungent smell and a strong bite to its taste. It adds richness to pasta dishes but you can choose a milder-flavored blue cheese, if you prefer a more subtle taste.

CHEDDAR comes in various strengths including mild, semi-matured (medium), matured (sharp) and vintage (extra sharp). The milder ones are paler yellow in color. They are all quite firm but the more mature ones are often more crumbly. All the cheddars are interchangeable.

HERBS

Basil, oregano, rosemary, sage, thyme and parsley are some of the herbs commonly found in pasta recipes. When herbs are stated in recipes, you should consider them as suggestions. If you prefer a different herb, or combination of herbs, experiment and develop your own recipes.

The amount of herbs used for any recipe is also a matter of personal taste. Substitute fresh herbs for dried if you wish but you need about three times as much when using fresh as they are not as strong as dried. Most herbs grow easily in sunny spots in the garden or in hanging baskets or pots.

DRIED PASTA

Dried pasta is commercially prepared and packaged, made from flour, water and salt and sometimes egg. Some shapes are especially suited to a particular type of sauce. Here we have given a guide to suitable sauces but you do not have to stick to any strict rules—it's your choice.

Below: Tagliatelle
(best with thin
coating sauces)

Right: Tomato tagliatelle
(excellent with thin
coating sauces)

Left: Penne
(best with thick or
chunky sauces)

Left: Rigatoni
(best with
chunky or thick
sauces)

Right: Lasagna
(layered with
sauces and baked)

Below: Conchiglie or
shells
(best with chunky
sauces which get trapped
in shells)

Above: Fettuccine
(excellent with thin
coating sauces)

Left: Orzo
(added to soups, casseroles)

Left: Linguine (best with thin coating sauces)

Left: Fusilli (best with sauces which get trapped in grooves)

Left: Orecchiette (best with sauces which get trapped in grooves)

Above: Spiral pasta (best with sauces which get trapped in grooves)

Right: Spaghetti (best with thin coating sauces or bolognese)

Below: Macaroni (best in baked dishes, soups)

Left: Spinach tagliatelle (best with thin coating sauces)

Above: Cannelloni (stuffed with filling and baked in a sauce)

Above: Farfalle or butterflies (best with sauces which get trapped in grooves)

Above: Tortellini shapes (excellent with sauces which get trapped in grooves)

Above: Ziti (suitable for thick or thin sauces)

Above right: Miniature star-shaped pasta (best for soups)

Above: Macaroni elbows (best in baked dishes, soups)

FRESH PASTA

Specialty pasta shops and some supermarkets and delicatessens stock fresh pasta. Some are flavored with herbs and spices or colored with vegetables. Fresh pasta cooks a lot more quickly than dried pasta. Here we have suggested types of sauces for each pasta.

Right: Lasagna sheets (layered with thick sauces and baked)

Above: Ravioli (excellent with mild-flavored thin sauces)

Below: Pumpkin gnocchi (best with thin sauces)

Left: Tortellini (best with mild-flavored thin sauces)

Below: Gnocchi (excellent with thin sauces)

Left: Cracked pepper tagliatelle (best with thin coating sauces)

Below: Pumpkin ravioli
(best with mild-flavored
thin sauces)

Below right: Spinach gnocchi
(best with thin coating sauces)

Below right: Tomato tagliatelle
Below left: Spinach tagliatelle
(both are best with thin
coating sauces)

Left: Spaghetti (best with thin
coating sauces or bolognese)

Above: Spinach tortellini
(excellent with thin sauces)

Above: Pappardelle
(suitable for thick,
thin or chunky sauces)

9

BASIC SAUCES

TOMATO AND OLIVE SAUCE

Preparation time: 25 minutes
Total cooking time: 15 minutes
Serves 4–6

2 lb large ripe tomatoes
1 tablespoon olive oil
2 cloves garlic, crushed
1 medium onion, finely chopped
1 lb penne, spaghetti,
   fettuccine or pasta of your
   choice

1/2 cup pitted black olives
2 teaspoons brown sugar
1 teaspoon red wine vinegar
salt and pepper to taste

➤ MARK A SMALL CROSS in the top of each tomato.
1 Place tomatoes in boiling water for 1–2 minutes; plunge in cold water. Peel skin down from the cross, discard skin. Chop tomatoes. Heat oil in a heavy-based pan. Add garlic and onion and cook, stirring, for 5 minutes over low heat.
2 Add tomatoes, cook, stirring, for 2–3

minutes. Allow to cool slightly. While waiting for sauce to cool, add pasta to large pan of boiling water and cook until just tender. Drain; return to pan.
3 To cooled sauce, add olives, sugar, vinegar, salt and pepper; stir until combined. Add sauce to pasta and toss to combine. Serve.

COOK'S FILE

Storage time: This sauce can be made up to one day in advance and refrigerated in an airtight container.
Note: If you prefer, you can puree mixture to a smooth consistency.

TOMATO SAUCE

Preparation time: 15 minutes
Total cooking time: 20 minutes
Serves 4–6

3 lb large ripe tomatoes
1 tablespoon olive oil
2 cloves garlic, crushed
1 onion, chopped
1 medium carrot, finely chopped
2 tablespoons tomato paste
1 teaspoon sugar
salt and pepper to taste

¼ cup freshly chopped mixed
   oregano, parsley and basil
1 lb rigatoni, penne, spaghetti or
   pasta of your choice

➤ MARK A SMALL CROSS in the
top of each tomato.
1 Place tomatoes in boiling water for
1–2 minutes; plunge into cold water.
Remove; peel skin down from cross.
Discard skin; roughly chop tomatoes.
2 Heat oil in heavy-based pan. Add
garlic and onion; cook 5 minutes over
low heat. Add tomatoes and carrot;
cook, stirring occasionally, for 10 min-

utes. Add tomato paste, sugar, salt and
pepper. Bring to boil; cook 2 minutes.
3 Place mixture in a food processor
and process briefly until sauce reaches
desired consistency. Add herbs and
stir to combine. While sauce is cooking, add pasta to a large pan of rapidly boiling water and cook until just
tender. Drain and return to pan. Add
sauce to pasta; toss well.

COOK'S FILE

Storage time: Sauce may be stored,
covered, in the refrigerator for up to
3 days or frozen for up to 3 months.

GARLIC SAUCE WITH PARSLEY

Preparation time: 10 minutes
Total cooking time: 15 minutes
Serves 4–6

4 cloves garlic
1 lb fusilli or spiral pasta
1 cup olive oil
1/4 cup chopped parsley
salt and pepper to taste

► CRUSH OR FINELY chop garlic into small bowl.

1 Add pasta to a large pan of boiling water and cook until just tender. Drain pasta and return to pan.

2 About five minutes before pasta is cooked, heat oil in heavy-based pan over low heat. Add garlic to pan; cook 30 seconds or until garlic is soft.

3 Pour oil and garlic over hot pasta. Add chopped parsley, salt and pepper; toss until pasta is well coated. Serve immediately.

C O O K ' S   F I L E

Hint: Cook the garlic until golden brown but not any darker as it will turn bitter.

Buy fresh plump garlic, not old, dried out bulbs.

Variations: Add 1 cup chopped olives with the parsley.

Add 2 tablespoons of chopped fresh oregano, basil, chives or sage with the parsley.

Add 4 chopped anchovies when cooking the garlic.

25 MINUTE BOLOGNESE

Preparation time: 10 minutes
Total cooking time: 25 minutes
Serves 4–6

1 tablespoon olive oil
1 medium onion, chopped
2 slices bacon, chopped
1 medium carrot, grated
1 1/2 lb ground beef
1/2 cup tomato paste

16 oz can crushed tomatoes
1 teaspoon dried mixed herbs
salt and pepper to taste
1 lb spaghetti or tagliatelle

➤ HEAT OIL IN A large deep pan. Add onion, bacon and carrot and stir for 5 minutes over medium heat.

1 Add ground beef, breaking up any lumps with the back of a fork. Cook until meat is well browned.

2 Stir in tomato paste, undrained crushed tomatoes and mixed herbs.

Bring to boil; reduce heat and simmer, uncovered, 15 minutes or until meat is tender. Add salt and pepper.

3 While sauce is cooking, add pasta to a large pan of boiling water and cook until just tender. Drain well. Serve sauce over pasta. Sprinkle with Parmesan cheese, if desired.

COOK'S FILE

Note: If you don't like a strong herb taste, use chopped fresh herbs of your choice—use about 2 tablespoons.

BOLOGNESE SAUCE

Preparation time: 15 minutes
Total cooking time: 1 hour 30 minutes
Serves 4–6

2 tablespoons olive oil
2 cloves garlic, crushed
1 large onion, chopped
1 medium carrot, chopped
1 stalk celery, chopped
1 lb ground beef
2 cups beef stock
1¹/₂ cups red wine
2 x 16 oz can crushed tomatoes
1 teaspoon sugar
2 tablespoons chopped fresh
    parsley

salt and pepper to taste
1 lb spaghetti or tagliatelle
2 tablespoons freshly grated
    Parmesan cheese, for serving

➤ HEAT OIL in a large deep pan.
1 Add garlic, onion, carrot and celery. Cook, stirring, for 5 minutes over
low heat until golden.
2 Increase heat; add beef, breaking it
up with a fork as it cooks. Stir until well
browned. Add stock, wine, undrained,
crushed tomatoes, sugar and parsley.
3 Bring to boil; reduce heat and simmer uncovered for 1¹/₂ hours, stirring

occasionally. Add salt and pepper.
Before sauce has finished cooking,
add pasta to a pan of rapidly boiling
water; cook until just tender. Drain
well. Serve sauce over top of pasta.
Sprinkle with Parmesan cheese.

COOK'S FILE

Note: Sauce can be used cold for layering lasagna. Make 1 day in advance
and store, covered, in refrigerator.

PESTO SAUCE

Preparation time: 10 minutes
Total cooking time: None
Serves 4–6

1 lb tagliatelle or fettuccine
¼ cup pine nuts
2 cups basil leaves
2 cloves garlic, crushed
½ teaspoon salt
¼ cup freshly grated Parmesan cheese
2 tablespoons freshly grated pecorino cheese (optional)
½ cup olive oil
black pepper to taste

➤ ADD PASTA to a large pan of rapidly boiling water and cook until just tender. Drain and return to pan.

1 About 5 minutes before pasta is cooked, add pine nuts to a heavy-based pan and stir over low heat for 2–3 minutes or until golden. Cool.
2 Place pine nuts, basil leaves, garlic and salt in food processor and process for 10 seconds. Scrape down sides of the bowl.
3 Add cheeses, process for 10 seconds. With motor running, gradually add oil until a paste is formed. Add pepper. Add to warm pasta and toss until sauce coats pasta.

COOK'S FILE

Storage time: Pesto sauce can be made up to 1 week in advance and stored in an airtight container in the refrigerator.

FAST PASTA

SPAGHETTI WITH PEAS AND BABY ONIONS

Preparation time: 10 minutes
Total cooking time: 15–20 minutes
Serves 4–6

1 lb spaghetti or vermicelli
2 bunches baby onions
1 tablespoon olive oil
4 slices bacon, chopped
2 teaspoons all-purpose flour
1 cup light chicken stock
1/2 cup white wine
1 cup shelled fresh green peas
ground black pepper to taste
fresh oregano sprigs, for
    garnish, optional

➤ ADD PASTA to a large pan of rapidly boiling water and cook until just tender. Drain pasta well and return to pan.

1 While pasta is cooking, trim outer skins and ends from baby onions, leaving only a small section of the green stem attached.

2 Heat oil in a large heavy-based deep pan. Add chopped bacon and trimmed onions and stir over low heat for 4 minutes or until golden. Sprinkle flour lightly over the top and stir for 1 minute.

3 Add combined stock and wine; increase heat and bring to boil.

4 Add shelled peas and cook for 5 minutes or until onions are tender. Add black pepper. Add mixture to pasta and toss gently. Serve in warmed pasta bowls. Garnish with oregano sprigs, if desired.

COOK'S FILE

Hints: Oregano is easy to grow so plant some in your garden or in pots.

If fresh peas are not available, use frozen ones.

Very small pickling onions can be used if baby onions are not available.

Variation: Vegetable stock can be used instead of chicken stock.

FETTUCCINE WITH SPINACH AND PROSCIUTTO

Preparation time: 10 minutes
Total cooking time: 10–15 minutes
Serves 4–6

1 lb spinach or plain fettuccine
2 tablespoons olive oil
8 thin slices prosciutto, chopped
3 scallions, chopped
1 bunch spinach
1 tablespoon balsamic vinegar

½ teaspoon sugar
salt and pepper to taste
½ cup freshly grated Parmesan cheese, for serving

➤ ADD PASTA to a large pan of rapidly boiling water and cook until just tender. Drain and return to pan.

1 While pasta is cooking, heat oil in a large heavy-based deep pan. Add prosciutto and scallions and cook, stirring occasionally, over medium heat for 5 minutes or until crisp.

2 Trim stalks from spinach, roughly chop leaves and add them to pan. Stir

in vinegar and sugar, cover and cook for 1 minute or until spinach has softened. Add salt and pepper.

3 Add the sauce to pasta and toss well to distribute the sauce evenly. Sprinkle with Parmesan and serve immediately.

COOK'S FILE

Storage time: This dish should be served as soon as it is cooked as the spinach turns an unattractive dull dark green if left standing.

Variation: Smoked bacon can be used instead of prosciutto.

FETTUCCINE WITH ZUCCHINI

Preparation time: 15 minutes
Total cooking time: 15 minutes
Serves 4–6

1 lb tagliatelle or fettuccine
1/3 cup butter
2 cloves garlic, crushed
1 lb zucchini, grated
3/4 cup freshly grated Parmesan
cheese

1 cup olive oil
16 medium-sized basil leaves

➤ COOK PASTA in a large pan of rapidly boiling water until just tender. Drain and return to pan.

1 While pasta is cooking, heat butter in a deep heavy-based pan over low heat until butter is foaming. Add garlic and cook for 1 minute. Add zucchini and cook, stirring occasionally, for 1–2 minutes or until softened.

2 Add zucchini sauce to pasta. Add Parmesan cheese and toss well.

3 To make basil leaves crisp, heat the oil in a small pan, add 2 leaves at a time and cook for 1 minute or until crisp. Remove with a slotted spoon and drain on paper towels. Repeat with remaining basil leaves. Divide pasta between warmed serving bowls, garnish with crisp basil leaves and serve immediately.

COOK'S FILE

Hint: Basil leaves can be fried up to 2 hours in advance. Store in an air-tight container after cooling.

LINGUINE WITH RED PEPPER SAUCE

Preparation time: 20 minutes
Total cooking time: 30 minutes
Serves 4–6

3 medium red peppers
3 tablespoons olive oil
1 large onion, sliced
2 cloves garlic, crushed
$1/4$–$1/2$ teaspoon chili flakes
 or powder
$1/2$ cup heavy cream
salt and pepper to taste
2 tablespoons chopped fresh
 oregano

1 lb linguine or spaghetti, plain
 or spinach

➤ HALVE EACH PEPPER and use a sharp knife to remove all the membrane and seeds.

1 Place the peppers cut-side down under a hot broiler and cook for 8 minutes or until black and blistered. Cover with a damp dish towel and allow to cool. Peel off skin and cut the peppers into thin strips.

2 Heat the oil in large heavy-based pan. Add the sliced onion and cook, stirring, over low heat for 8 minutes or until the onions are soft. Add peppers, garlic, chili and cream, cook for 2 minutes, stirring occasionally.

Add the salt, pepper and chopped oregano.

3 Before the sauce is cooked, add the pasta to a large pan of rapidly boiling water and cook until it is just tender. Drain the pasta well and return it to the pan. Add the sauce to the hot pasta and toss well until evenly combined. Serve in warmed pasta bowls.

COOK'S FILE

Hint: If necessary, you can substitute dried oregano—use about one-third of the quantity as dried herbs have a much stronger flavor.
Variation: For a stronger pepper flavor, omit the cream.

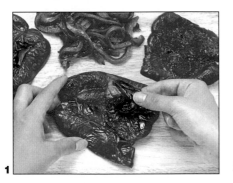

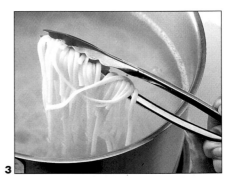

SPIRALS WITH GREEN SAUCE

Preparation time: 10 minutes
Total cooking time: 15 minutes
Serves 4–6

1 lb fusilli or spiral pasta
1 medium onion
2 medium zucchini
5–6 large swiss chard leaves
2 anchovies
1 tablespoon capers
2 tablespoons olive oil
$1/4$ cup butter

$1/4$ cup white wine
salt and pepper to taste

➤ ADD PASTA to a large pan of boiling water and cook until just tender. Drain and return to pan.

1 While pasta is cooking, chop onion finely. Grate the zucchini into fine pieces. Remove and discard stalks from swiss chard. Chop or shred leaves into small pieces. Chop anchovies and capers finely. Heat olive oil and butter in a large heavy-based deep pan. Add prepared onion and zucchini, stir with a wooden spoon for 3 minutes over medium heat.

2 Add anchovies, capers, wine, salt and pepper to pan and cook, stirring, for 2 minutes.

3 Add prepared swiss chard to pan and cook for 1–2 minutes or until swiss chard has softened. Add Green Sauce to warm pasta and toss until well distributed through sauce. Serve in warmed pasta bowls.

COOK'S FILE

Note: Filleted anchovies are available canned in oil or salted in jars.
Variation: Use a whole bunch of spinach instead of swiss chard. Cut ends off; shred into small pieces.

Linguine with Red Pepper Sauce (top) and Spirals with Green Sauce

GRILLED PEPPER AND ANCHOVY SALAD

Preparation time: 15 minutes
Total cooking time: 25 minutes
Serves 4–6

1 lb penne or spiral pasta
1 small red onion
2 large red peppers
1 cup fresh flat-leaf parsley
     leaves
2 anchovies, whole or chopped
1/4 cup olive oil
2 tablespoons lemon juice
salt and pepper to taste

➤ ADD PENNE OR SPIRAL pasta to a large pan of rapidly boiling water and cook until just tender.

1 Drain pasta immediately and rinse well under cold water. Peel onion and chop finely.

2 Cut peppers in half and remove seeds and membrane. Place them cut-side down under a hot broiler and cook for 8 minutes or until skin is blistered and black. Remove to a plate and cover with a damp dish towel. When they are cool, peel the skin away and cut pepper flesh into thin strips.

3 In a large salad bowl, combine pasta, pepper strips, onion, parsley, anchovies, oil, lemon juice, salt and pepper. Toss until well combined and serve immediately.

COOK'S FILE

Hints: To prevent pasta sticking together, after rinsing under cold water add a little of the oil to pasta and toss well.

Peppers can be prepared 1 day in advance, covered well and refrigerated. Removing the skin in this way results in a sweeter taste from the pepper.

SPAGHETTI TOMATO SALAD

Preparation time: 25 minutes
Total cooking time: 15 minutes
Serves 4–6

1 lb spaghettini or spaghetti
1 cup fresh basil leaves
8 oz cherry tomatoes, halved
1 clove garlic, crushed
$^1/_2$ cup chopped black olives

$^1/_4$ cup olive oil
1 tablespoon balsamic vinegar
$^1/_2$ cup freshly grated Parmesan cheese
salt and pepper to taste

➤ ADD PASTA to a large pan of rapidly boiling water and cook until just tender. Drain pasta and rinse well under cold water.

1 Using a sharp knife, chop basil leaves into fine strips.

2 In a bowl combine basil, tomatoes, garlic, olives, oil and vinegar. Allow to stand for 15 minutes. Place drained pasta in a large salad bowl and add tomato mixture.

3 Add Parmesan, salt and pepper. Toss well and serve immediately.

COOK'S FILE

Storage time: Pasta can be cooked up to 1 day in advance. If doing this, cool pasta and toss with a little oil.

Note: Balsamic vinegar is an aged vinegar from Modena, Italy. It is available in most supermarkets and specialty food stores.

1

2

3

FARFALLE SALAD WITH SUN-DRIED TOMATOES AND SPINACH

Preparation time: 20 minutes
Total cooking time: 12 minutes
Serves 4–6

1 lb farfalle (butterfly pasta) or spiral pasta
3 scallions
1²/₃ oz sun-dried tomatoes, cut into strips
1 bunch spinach, stalks trimmed and leaves shredded
¹/₃ cup toasted pine nuts
1 tablespoon chopped fresh oregano

Dressing
¹/₄ cup olive oil
1 teaspoon fresh chopped chili
1 clove garlic, crushed
salt and pepper to taste

➤ ADD PASTA to a large pan of rapidly boiling water and cook until just tender. Drain pasta and rinse well under cold water. Transfer to a large salad bowl.

1 Trim scallions and chop finely. Add to pasta with tomato, spinach, pine nuts and oregano.

2 To make Dressing: Combine oil, chili, garlic, salt and pepper in a small screwtop jar and shake well.

3 Pour dressing over the top of salad; toss well and serve.

COOK'S FILE

Storage time: Serve immediately.

1

2

3

ITALIAN OMELET

Preparation time: 20 minutes
Total cooking time: 15 minutes
Serves 4

2 tablespoons olive oil
1 onion, finely chopped
4 oz ham, sliced
6 eggs
1/4 cup milk
salt and freshly ground black
   pepper to taste

2 cups cooked fusilli or spiral
   pasta (4³/4 oz uncooked)
1/4 cup freshly grated Parmesan
   cheese
2 tablespoons chopped fresh
   parsley
1 tablespoon chopped fresh basil
1/2 cup freshly grated cheddar
   cheese

➤ HEAT HALF the oil in pan. Add
onion; stir over low heat until tender.
1 Add sliced ham to pan and stir for
1 minute. Transfer to a plate.

2 In a bowl, whisk eggs, milk, salt
and pepper. Stir in pasta, Parmesan,
herbs and onion mixture.
3 Heat remaining oil in same pan.
Pour egg mixture into pan. Sprinkle
with cheddar cheese. Cook over medium heat until mixture begins to set
around the edges. Place under a hot
broiler to complete the cooking. Cut
into wedges for serving.

COOK'S FILE

Hint: Serve with crisp green or mixed
salad, if desired.

PASTA WITH RICOTTA, CHILI AND HERBS

Preparation time: 15 minutes
Total cooking time: 20 minutes
Serves 4

1 lb spiral pasta or penne
1/4 cup olive oil
3 cloves garlic, crushed
2 teaspoons very finely chopped
    fresh chili

1 cup fresh flat-leaf parsley
    leaves, roughly chopped
1/2 cup fresh basil leaves,
    shredded
1/2 cup fresh oregano leaves,
    roughly chopped
salt and pepper to taste
6 1/2 oz fresh ricotta cheese, cut
    into small cubes

➤ ADD PASTA to a large pan of
rapidly boiling water and cook until
just tender. Drain and return to pan.

1 When pasta is almost cooked, heat
oil in a non-stick heavy-based frying
pan. Add garlic and chili to pan and
stir for 1 minute over low heat.
2 Add oil mixture, herbs, salt and
pepper to pasta. Toss well until mixture coats pasta thoroughly.
3 Add cubes of ricotta and serve
immediately.

COOK'S FILE

Note: Fresh ricotta is firm and is sold
in delicatessens. Use within 2 days.

1

2

3

GREEN OLIVE AND EGGPLANT TOSS

Preparation time: 20 minutes
Total cooking time: 20 minutes
Serves 4

1 lb fettuccine or tagliatelle
1 cup green olives
1 large eggplant
2 tablespoons olive oil
2 cloves garlic, crushed

¹/₂ cup lemon juice
salt and pepper to taste
2 tablespoons chopped fresh
  parsley
¹/₂ cup freshly grated Parmesan
  cheese

➤ ADD PASTA to a large pan of rapidly boiling water and cook until just tender. Drain and return to pan.

1 While pasta is cooking, chop olives and cut eggplant into small cubes.

2 Heat oil in a heavy-based frying pan. Add garlic; stir for 30 seconds. Add eggplant and cook over medium heat, stirring frequently, for 6 minutes or until tender.

3 Add olives, lemon juice, salt and pepper to pan. Add sauce to pasta and toss. Serve in warmed pasta bowls. Sprinkle with parsley and cheese.

COOK'S FILE

Hint: To draw out bitter juices, eggplant can be salted, left to stand for 30 minutes, then rinsed well before using.

Spaghetti with Arugula and Chili

Tagliatelle with Herb Sauce

Spiral Pasta with Bread Crumb Sauce

PRONTO PASTA

SPAGHETTI WITH ARUGULA AND CHILI

Add 1 lb spaghetti or spaghettini to a large pan of rapidly boiling water and cook until just tender. Drain and return to pan. Five minutes before pasta is cooked, heat 2 tablespoons olive oil in a large heavy-based frying pan. Add 2 teaspoons chopped chili and cook for 1 minute over low heat, stirring. Add 3 bunches trimmed arugula and cook for 2–3 minutes or until softened, stirring regularly. Add 1 tablespoon lemon juice and salt to taste. Add sauce to pasta and toss until mixed. Serve immediately. Serves 4–6.

SPIRAL PASTA WITH BREAD CRUMB SAUCE

Process 5 slices brown bread in a food processor for 30 seconds or until it forms fine crumbs. Add 1 lb spiral pasta or farfalle to a large pan of rapidly boiling water and cook until just tender. Drain, keep warm. While pasta is cooking, heat $1/4$ cup olive oil in a large heavy-based frying pan over low heat. Add bread crumbs and 3 cloves crushed garlic and stir 3 minutes or until crisp and golden. Combine hot pasta, bread crumbs, 2 tablespoons finely chopped parsley and $1/2$ cup freshly grated pecorino cheese in a large serving bowl. Add ground black pepper to taste. Toss well and serve immediately. Garnish with fresh herbs, if desired. Serves 4–6.

*Shells with Artichoke,
Salami and Tomato*

*Lasagnette with Spinach
and Mushroom Sauce*

LASAGNETTE WITH SPINACH
AND MUSHROOM SAUCE

Add 1 lb lasagnette or pappardelle to a large pan of rapidly
boiling water and cook until just tender. Drain and return
to pan. While pasta is cooking, heat 2 tablespoons olive oil
and 1/4 cup butter in a large heavy-based pan over medium heat. Add 3 chopped scallions and 8 oz sliced baby
mushrooms and cook for 5 minutes, stirring occasionally,
over medium heat. Add 1 bunch spinach, stems removed
and leaves shredded, and cook 2 minutes or until spinach
is just tender. Add salt and pepper to taste. Add sauce to
pasta and toss until combined. Divide pasta between
warmed serving bowls. Garnish with freshly grated
Parmesan and serve immediately. Serves 4–6.

TAGLIATELLE WITH HERB SAUCE

Add 1 lb tagliatelle or trenette to a large pan of rapidly
boiling water and cook until just tender. Drain and return
to pan. While pasta is cooking, place 1 1/2 cups fresh parsley leaves, 1 cup fresh basil leaves, 1/2 cup fresh oregano
and 1/4 cup toasted pine nuts in food processor and
process for 10 seconds or until finely chopped. With motor
running, add 1/2 cup olive oil and process for 10 seconds or
until a smooth paste is formed. Add salt and pepper to
taste. Add sauce to pasta and toss well. Serve immediately,
garnished with shavings of fresh Parmesan cheese,
if desired. Serves 4–6.

SHELLS WITH ARTICHOKE,
SALAMI AND TOMATO

Add 1 lb shells or spiral pasta to a large pan of rapidly
boiling water and cook until just tender. Drain, keep warm.
Heat 2 tablespoons olive oil in a large heavy-based frying
pan; add 6 slices salami, cut into strips, and stir for
2 minutes over medium heat. Stir in 10 sundried tomatoes
(4 3/4 oz), cut into strips. Drain a 14 oz can artichoke hearts,
cut artichokes into wedges. Add to pan with black pepper
to taste, and 2 tablespoons each of chopped fresh basil and
parsley; cook for 1 minute. Divide pasta between warmed
serving bowls and top with sauce. Serves 4–6.

SOUPS

BEAN SOUP WITH SAUSAGE

Preparation time: 25 minutes
Total cooking time: 25 minutes
Serves 4–6

4 Italian sausage links
2 teaspoons olive oil
2 medium leeks, sliced
1 clove garlic, crushed
1 large carrot, chopped into cubes
2 stalks celery, sliced
2 tablespoons all-purpose flour
2 beef bouillon cubes, crumbled
8 cups hot water
1/2 cup white wine
4 oz small shell pasta
15 oz can desired bean or combination of beans, (such as pinto, kidney or butter) drained
1 teaspoon chopped chili (optional)
salt and pepper to taste

➤ CUT SAUSAGE links into pieces.

1 Heat oil in large heavy-based pan, add sausage pieces. Cook over medium heat for 5 minutes or until golden, stirring regularly. Remove from pan and drain on paper towels.

2 Add leek, garlic, carrot and celery to pan, cook for 2–3 minutes or until soft, stirring occasionally.

3 Add flour, cook 1 minute stirring constantly. Add bouillon cubes; stir in water and wine. Bring to boil; reduce heat; simmer uncovered, 10 minutes.

4 Add pasta, beans and chili to pan. Increase heat; cook 8–10 minutes or until pasta is tender. Return sausage to pan, add salt and pepper. Serve with chopped fresh parsley, if desired.

COOK'S FILE

Variation: Use dried beans, if preferred. Place in bowl; cover with water; soak overnight. Drain; add to large pan with water to come about 1¼ inches above beans; simmer 1 hour. Drain well before adding to soup.

MINESTRONE WITH PESTO

Preparation time: 25 minutes
Total cooking time: 30 minutes
Serves 4–6

2 medium onions, chopped
1 green pepper, membrane and
    seeds removed, chopped
2 large zucchini, sliced
1 small eggplant, chopped
2 large carrots, chopped
8 cups water
2 beef bouillon cubes, crumbled
1 cup frozen green peas

15 oz can red kidney beans,
    drained
8 oz miniature pasta
1/4 cup chopped fresh parsley
salt and pepper to taste
2 tablespoons freshly grated
    Parmesan cheese, for serving

Pesto
2 cloves garlic, crushed
2 cups fresh basil leaves
1/2 cup freshly grated Parmesan
    cheese
1/2 cup olive oil

➤ PLACE THE PREPARED onion, pepper, zucchini, eggplant and carrot in hot water in large deep pan.
1 Add crumbled bouillon cubes. Bring to boil over high heat; reduce heat and simmer for 20 minutes, stirring occasionally.
2 Add peas, beans, pasta and parsley. Cook for 10 minutes or until pasta is just tender. Add salt and pepper and serve with Pesto. Sprinkle with freshly grated Parmesan cheese.
3 To make Pesto: Combine garlic, basil, cheese and oil in a food processor and process for 10 seconds or until mixture forms a paste.

COOK'S FILE

Variation: Use chicken bouillon cubes.

1

2

3

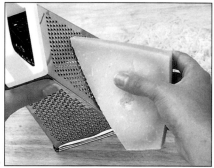

LEMON-SCENTED BROTH WITH TORTELLINI

Preparation time: 10 minutes
Total cooking time: 18 minutes
Serves 4–6

1 lemon
$^1/_2$ cup good quality white wine
10$^3/_4$ oz can condensed chicken broth
3 cups water
$^1/_3$ cup chopped fresh parsley
black pepper to taste
12 oz fresh or dried veal- or chicken-filled tortellini
2 tablespoons grated Parmesan

➤ USING A VEGETABLE peeler, peel wide strips from lemon.

1 Remove white pith with a small sharp knife and cut 3 of the wide pieces into fine strips; set aside the fine strips for garnish.

2 Place wide lemon strips, white wine, broth and water in a large deep pan. Cook for 10 minutes over low heat. Remove lemon rind from pan and bring mixture to boil.

3 Add 2 tablespoons of parsley, pepper and tortellini to pan. Cook for 6–7 minutes or until pasta is just tender. Garnish with remaining parsley and fine strips of lemon.

4 If desired, you can grate some Parmesan to sprinkle over the top.

COOK'S FILE

Storage time: If desired, the day before broth is required, follow recipe to the removal of lemon rind from pan. Just before serving, bring mixture to boil; add chopped parsley, black pepper and tortellini. Continue with recipe.

Variations: Use chopped fresh basil instead of parsley.

You can use different types of tortellini for this recipe.

COUNTRY SQUASH AND PASTA SOUP

Preparation time: 25 minutes
Total cooking time: 18 minutes
Serves 4–6

1 large onion
1 lb 6 1/2 oz winter squash
2 medium potatoes
1 tablespoon olive oil
2 tablespoons butter

2 cloves garlic, crushed
12 cups light chicken stock
4 oz miniature pasta or orzo
1 tablespoon chopped fresh
   parsley, for serving, optional

➤ PEEL ONION and chop finely.
1 Peel squash and potatoes and chop into small cubes. Heat oil and butter in a large pan. Add onion and garlic and cook, stirring, for 5 minutes over low heat.
2 Add squash, potato and chicken stock. Increase heat, cover pan and cook for 8 minutes or until vegetables are tender.
3 Add pasta and cook, stirring occasionally, for 5 minutes or until pasta is just tender. Serve immediately. Sprinkle with chopped parsley, if desired.

COOK'S FILE

Note: Butternut or acorn squash will give the sweetest flavor.

  Tiny star-shaped pasta look attractive in this soup.

BACON AND PEA SOUP

Preparation time: 20 minutes
Total cooking time: 15 minutes
Serves 4–6

1 large onion
4 slices thick bacon
1 tablespoon butter
1 stalk celery, chopped into
    small pieces
8 cups chicken stock

1 cup frozen green peas
8 oz orzo
2 tablespoons chopped fresh
    parsley
pepper to taste

➤ PEEL ONION and chop finely.
1 Trim rind and excess fat from bacon; chop bacon into small pieces.
2 Place bacon, butter, onion and celery in large heavy-based pan. Cook for 5 minutes over low heat, stirring occasionally. Add chicken stock and peas;

simmer, covered, 5 minutes. Increase heat and add orzo; cook, uncovered, stirring occasionally, for 5 minutes.
3 Add chopped parsley and pepper just before serving.

COOK'S FILE

Storage time: You can make this soup the day before required and store in an airtight container in refrigerator. Gently reheat before serving.
Hint: Double-smoked bacon will give the best flavor.

PASTA WITH TOMATO

SPAGHETTI PUTTANESCA

Preparation time: 15 minutes
Total cooking time: 20 minutes
Serves 4–6

1 lb spaghetti or fettuccine
2 tablespoons olive oil
3 cloves garlic, crushed
2 tablespoons chopped fresh
　parsley
1/4–1/2 teaspoon chili flakes or
　powder
2 x 16 oz cans crushed tomatoes
1 tablespoon capers
3 anchovies, chopped
1/4 cup black olives
black pepper to taste

➤ ADD SPAGHETTI or fettuccine to a large pan of rapidly boiling water.

1 Cook pasta until just tender and drain immediately. Return drained pasta to pan.
2 While pasta is cooking, heat oil in a heavy-based frying pan. Add garlic, parsley and chili flakes and cook, stirring, 1 minute over medium heat.
3 Add undrained, crushed tomatoes and stir to combine. Reduce heat and simmer, covered, for 5 minutes.
4 Add capers, anchovies and olives and cook, stirring, for 5 minutes. Add black pepper; stir. Add sauce to pasta and toss gently until evenly distributed. Serve immediately in warmed pasta bowls.

COOK'S FILE

Hint: You can leave tomatoes in the can and chop with a pair of kitchen scissors. Otherwise, drain them, reserving juice, and chop on a board.

BUCATINI WITH FARMHOUSE SAUCE

Preparation time: 20 minutes
Total cooking time: 25 minutes
Serves 4–6

2 tablespoons olive oil
8 oz mushrooms
1 medium eggplant
2 cloves garlic, crushed
28 oz can crushed tomatoes
1 lb bucatini or spaghetti

salt and pepper to taste
¼ cup chopped fresh parsley

➤ HEAT OIL in a medium heavy-based pan.
1 Wipe mushrooms with paper towels; slice. Chop eggplant into small cubes.
2 Add mushrooms, eggplant and garlic to pan and cook, stirring, for 4 minutes. Add undrained, crushed tomatoes; cover and simmer for 15 minutes. While sauce is cooking, add pasta to a large pan of rapidly boiling water and

cook until just tender. Drain and return to pan.
3 Season the sauce with salt and pepper. Add chopped parsley to pan and stir. Add sauce to the pasta and toss well. Serve immediately in warmed pasta bowls.

COOK'S FILE

Hint: If the pasta is cooked before you are ready to serve you can prevent it sticking together by adding a little olive oil after draining it. Toss oil through pasta.

RIGATONI WITH KIDNEY BEANS AND ITALIAN SAUSAGE

Preparation time: 25 minutes
Total cooking time: 30 minutes
Serves 4–6

1 tablespoon olive oil
1 large onion, chopped
2 cloves garlic, crushed
4 Italian sausage links, chopped
28 oz can crushed tomatoes
15 oz can red kidney beans, drained

2 tablespoons chopped fresh basil
1 tablespoon chopped fresh sage
1 tablespoon chopped fresh parsley
salt and pepper to taste
1 lb rigatoni or large shells
1/4 cup freshly grated Parmesan cheese, for serving

► HEAT OIL in a medium heavy-based pan.
1 Add onion, garlic and sausage to pan and cook, stirring occasionally, over medium heat for 5 minutes.
2 Add undrained, crushed tomatoes, beans, basil, sage, parsley, salt and pepper. Reduce heat and simmer for 20 minutes.
3 While sauce is cooking, add pasta to a large pan of boiling water and cook until just tender. Drain. Divide the pasta between warmed serving bowls, top with sauce. Sprinkle with grated Parmesan cheese and serve immediately.

COOK'S FILE

Hint: Dried beans may be used. Soak overnight in water; drain, place in a pan, cover with water, bring to boil and cook for 20 minutes or until tender.

PENNE WITH PROSCIUTTO

Preparation time: 15 minutes
Total cooking time: 25 minutes
Serves 4–6

1 medium onion
28 oz can tomatoes
1 tablespoon olive oil
6 thin slices prosciutto
   (approximately 2^{1}/$_{2}$ oz),
   chopped

1 tablespoon chopped fresh
   rosemary
salt and pepper to taste
1 lb penne or macaroni
^{1}/$_{2}$ cup freshly grated Parmesan
   cheese, for serving

➤ PEEL ONION and chop finely.
1 Using scissors, crush tomatoes while still in the can.
2 Heat oil in medium heavy-based frying pan. Add prosciutto and onion and cook, stirring occasionally, over low heat for 5 minutes or until golden.

3 Add rosemary, undrained tomatoes, salt and pepper; simmer for 10 minutes. While sauce is cooking, add pasta to a large pan of rapidly boiling water and cook until just tender. Drain. Divide pasta between warmed serving bowls and top with sauce. Sprinkle with Parmesan cheese and serve immediately.

COOK'S FILE

Note: Rosemary, commonly used in Mediterranean cookery, adds a distinctive flavor to this dish.

RIGATONI WITH AMATRICIANA SAUCE

Preparation time: 25 minutes
Total cooking time: 20 minutes
Serves 4–6

2 lb ripe red tomatoes
1 lb rigatoni
1 tablespoon olive oil
3 thin slices bacon or 6 thin
    slices pancetta, finely
    chopped
1 small onion, very finely
    choppcd
2 teaspoons very finely chopped
    fresh chili
salt and pepper to taste

➤ MARK A SMALL CROSS in the
bottom of each tomato.
1 Place tomatoes in boiling water for
1–2 minutes, then plunge into cold
water. Remove from water and peel
back skin from the cross. Roughly
chop tomatoes.
2 Add rigatoni to a large pan of
rapidly boiling water and cook until
just tender. Drain and return to pan.
Keep warm.
3 About 6 minutes before rigatoni is
cooked, heat oil in a heavy-based frying pan. Add bacon, onion and chili
and stir over medium heat for 3 minutes. Add tomatoes, salt and pepper.
Reduce heat and simmer for 3 minutes. Add sauce to pasta and toss
until well combined.

COOK'S FILE

Hint: Try Roma (plum) or egg tomatoes in this recipe—you'll find them
sometimes in supermarkets or grocers.
They are firm-fleshed, with few seeds
and a rich flavor. Use them in sauces
and for bottling and sun-drying—they
are particularly good.

SPAGHETTI SIRACUSANI

Preparation time: 15 minutes
Total cooking time: 1 hour
Serves 4–6

1 large green pepper
2 tablespoons olive oil
2 cloves garlic, crushed
2 x 16 oz cans crushed tomatoes
¹/₂ cup water
2 medium zucchini, chopped
2 anchovies, chopped
1 tablespoon capers, chopped

¹/₄ cup black olives, pitted and
  halved
2 tablespoons chopped fresh
  basil leaves
salt and pepper to taste
1 lb spaghetti or linguine
¹/₂ cup freshly grated Parmesan
  cheese, for serving

➤ REMOVE MEMBRANE and seeds
from pepper.
1 Slice into thin strips. Heat oil in a
large deep pan. Add garlic to pan and
stir for 30 seconds over low heat.
2 Add pepper, undrained, crushed

tomatoes, water, zucchini, anchovies,
capers and olives. Cook for 20 minutes, stirring occasionally.
3 Add basil, salt and pepper to pan
and stir. While sauce is cooking, add
pasta to a large pan of rapidly boiling
water; cook until just tender. Drain
thoroughly. Divide pasta between
warmed serving bowls and top with
sauce. Sprinkle with Parmesan and
serve immediately.

COOK'S FILE

Storage time: Sauce can be made
1 day in advance.

TAGLIATELLE WITH SWEET TOMATO AND WALNUT SAUCE

Preparation time: 20 minutes
Total cooking time: 45 minutes
Serves 4–6

4 ripe tomatoes
1 medium carrot
1 tablespoon oil
1 medium onion, finely
   chopped
1 stalk celery, finely chopped
2 tablespoons chopped fresh
   parsley
1 teaspoon red wine vinegar
1/4 cup white wine
salt and pepper to taste
1 lb tagliatelle or fettuccine
1 tablespoon olive oil, extra
3/4 cup walnuts, roughly chopped
1/3 cup freshly grated Parmesan
   cheese, for serving

➤ MARK A SMALL CROSS on the bottom of each tomato.

1 Place tomatoes in boiling water for 1–2 minutes, then plunge into cold water. Peel skin down from cross, roughly chop tomatoes. Peel and grate the carrot.

2 Heat oil in a large heavy-based pan and cook onion and celery for 5 minutes over low heat, stirring regularly. Add tomatoes, carrot, parsley and combined vinegar and wine. Reduce heat and simmer for 25 minutes. Season to taste.

3 While sauce is cooking, add pasta to a large pan of rapidly boiling water and cook until just tender. Drain and return to pan. Add sauce to pasta and toss to combine.

4 Five minutes before sauce is cooked, heat extra oil in a medium frying pan, stir walnuts over low heat for 5 minutes. Serve pasta and sauce topped with walnuts and sprinkled with Parmesan cheese.

COOK'S FILE

Hints: It is handy to have fresh parsley on hand for use in cookery so try growing your own. You'll find it grows easily in the garden or in pots.

   Pasta comes in different widths and thicknesses so choose whichever type you prefer.

   The Italians often use Roma (plum) or egg tomatoes when cooking sauces, try them if they are available. You'll need about 6–8 as they are small.

SPAGHETTI AND MUSSELS IN TOMATO AND HERB SAUCE

Preparation time: 15 minutes
Total cooking time: 30 minutes
Serves 4

1 onion
3 lb mussels in the shell
2 tablespoons olive oil
2 cloves garlic, crushed
16 oz can crushed tomatoes
1 cup white wine
1 tablespoon chopped fresh basil

2 tablespoons chopped fresh
  parsley
salt and freshly ground black
  pepper to taste
1 lb spaghetti

➤ PEEL ONION and slice finely.
1 Remove beards from mussels and wash away any grit. Set aside.
2 Heat oil in a large pan. Add onion and crushed garlic; stir over low heat until onion is tender. Add undrained, crushed tomatoes, wine, basil, parsley, salt and pepper. Bring to boil. Reduce heat and simmer for 15–20 minutes or until sauce begins to thicken.

3 Add prepared mussels to pan. Cook, covered, for about 5 minutes, shaking the pan occasionally. Discard any mussels that do not open. While sauce is cooking, add the spaghetti to a large pan of rapidly boiling water and cook until just tender. Drain immediately. Serve mussels and sauce over pasta.

COOK'S FILE

Hints: Serve with crusty bread and a crisp green salad.
  If fresh herbs are unavailable you can substitute about one-third the amount of dried.

PASTA MARINARA

Preparation time: 10 minutes
Total cooking time: 20 minutes
Serves 4

8 oz boneless fish fillets
1 large calamari tube
1 tablespoon olive oil
1 onion, sliced
1 clove garlic, crushed
1/2 cup red wine
2 tablespoons tomato paste
16 oz can crushed tomatoes
1 tablespoon chopped fresh
  basil
1/4 teaspoon dried oregano

salt and freshly ground black
  pepper to taste
5 oz medium raw shrimp,
  peeled, deveined (leave tails
  intact)
4 oz scallops, halved
4 oz mussel meat, optional
1 lb linguine

➤ CUT FISH FILLETS into small even-sized pieces.
1 Thinly slice calamari. Heat oil in a large frying pan. Add onion and garlic; stir over low heat until onion is tender. Add wine and tomato paste; stir to combine. Simmer until liquid is reduced by half. Add undrained, crushed tomatoes and stir.

2 Add basil, oregano, salt and pepper. Simmer gently for 10 minutes, stirring occasionally.
3 Add prepared fish, calamari, shrimp, scallops and mussel meat to tomato sauce. Simmer, stirring, for 2–3 minutes or until flesh changes color. While sauce is cooking, add pasta to a large pan of rapidly boiling water and cook until just tender. Drain well. Serve sauce over pasta.

COOK'S FILE

Hints: Use the small bay scallops, not the large sea scallops, for this recipe.
  Overcooking of seafood will cause it to toughen.

Spaghetti and Mussels in Tomato and Herb Sauce (top) and
Pasta Marinara

LINGUINE WITH ANCHOVIES, OLIVES AND CAPERS

Preparation time: 15 minutes
Total cooking time: 20 minutes
Serves 4

1 lb linguine
2 tablespoons olive oil
2 cloves garlic, crushed
2 tomatoes, peeled and chopped (optional)
1/4 cup capers
1/2 cup chopped pitted black olives
1/4 cup chopped pitted green olives
1/4 cup dry white wine
1/4 cup chopped fresh flat-leaf parsley or basil
freshly ground black pepper, to taste
2 x 2 oz cans anchovies, drained and chopped

➤ ADD LINGUINE to a large pan of rapidly boiling water and cook until just tender. Drain well. Return pasta to pan; keep warm.

1 While pasta is cooking, heat oil in a frying pan. Add garlic and stir over low heat for 1 minute. Add tomatoes, capers and olives; cook for 2 minutes.

2 Add wine, parsley and pepper and stir. Bring to boil; reduce heat and simmer for 5 minutes. Remove pan from heat.

3 Add anchovies to pan. Add sauce to warm pasta and toss to distribute sauce evenly through pasta. Serve immediately.

COOK'S FILE

Hint: In a pan, heat a little olive oil and add some fresh bread crumbs and a crushed clove of garlic; toss until crisp and golden. Sprinkle over pasta with Parmesan. This will add flavor and look attractive.

46

PASTA WITH CLAMS

Preparation time: 25 minutes
Total cooking time: 20 minutes
Serves 4

1 lb small shell pasta
2 lb clams
1 tablespoon olive oil
2 cloves garlic, crushed
2 x 16 oz cans crushed tomatoes
$1/4$ cup red wine
2 tablespoons chopped fresh
 parsley
1 teaspoon sugar
salt and freshly ground black
 pepper to taste

➤ HEAT A LARGE pan of water until water is boiling rapidly.

1 Add pasta and cook until just tender. Drain and keep warm. Blend 2 tablespoons each of salt and all-purpose flour with enough water to make a paste. Add to a large pan of cold water and soak shellfish in mixture overnight. This will draw out sand from inside shells. Scrub shells well. Rinse and drain.

2 Heat oil in a large pan. Add garlic and cook over low heat for 30 seconds. Add undrained, crushed tomatoes, wine, parsley, sugar, salt and pepper; stir. Bring to boil. Reduce heat and simmer, stirring occasionally, for 5 minutes.

3 Add scrubbed clams to pan. Cook over medium heat, stirring occasionally, until all shells have opened. Discard any that do not open. Divide pasta into warmed pasta bowls. Serve clams and sauce over pasta.

C O O K ' S   F I L E

Hints: If fresh clams are not available, use mussels, scallops or drained, canned clams instead.

SPAGHETTI WITH CHILI CALAMARI

Preparation time: 10 minutes
Total cooking time: 15 minutes
Serves 4

1 lb calamari, cleaned
1 lb spaghetti
2 tablespoons olive oil
1 leek, chopped
2 cloves garlic, crushed
1–2 teaspoons chopped chili
1/2 teaspoon cayenne pepper
16 oz can crushed tomatoes
1/2 cup fish stock

1 tablespoon chopped fresh basil
2 teaspoons chopped fresh sage
1 teaspoon chopped fresh marjoram

➤ PULL TENTACLES from body of calamari.

1 Using fingers pull quill from pouch of calamari. Pull skin away from flesh and discard. Using a sharp knife, slit the tubes up one side, lay out flat and score one side in a diamond pattern. Cut into four.

2 Add spaghetti to a large pan of rapidly boiling water and cook until just tender. Drain and keep warm. While pasta is cooking, heat oil in a large frying pan. Add leek and cook for 2 minutes. Add garlic and stir over low heat for 1 minute. Stir in chili and cayenne. Add undrained, crushed tomatoes, stock and herbs. Bring to boil. Reduce heat; simmer 5 minutes.

3 Add calamari to pan. Simmer for another 5–10 minutes or until tender. Serve Chili Calamari over spaghetti. Serve with salad, if desired.

COOK'S FILE

Note: Prepare fish stock by covering fish bones and roughly chopped onion, celery and carrot with water. Bring to boil. Reduce heat. Simmer for 30 minutes. Drain well. Use immediately.

1

2

3

TAGLIATELLE WITH OCTOPUS

Preparation time: 15 minutes
Total cooking time: 20 minutes
Serves 4

1 lb mixed tagliatelle
2 lb baby octopus
2 tablespoons olive oil
1 onion, sliced
1 clove garlic, crushed
15 oz can tomato puree
1/2 cup dry white wine
1 tablespoon chili sauce

1 tablespoon chopped fresh basil
salt and freshly ground black
pepper to taste

➤ ADD TAGLIATELLE to a large pan of rapidly boiling water and cook until just tender. Drain; keep warm.

1 Clean octopus (see Note) and cut them in half.

2 While pasta is cooking, heat oil in a large frying pan. Add onion and garlic and stir over low heat until onion is tender. Add tomato puree, wine, chili sauce, basil, salt and pepper to pan. Bring to boil. Reduce heat and simmer for 10 minutes.

3 Add octopus to the pan. Simmer mixture for 5–10 minutes or until tender. Pour octopus sauce over pasta and serve immediately.

COOK'S FILE

Note: To clean octopus, use a small sharp knife and remove the gut by either cutting off the head entirely or by slicing open the head and removing the gut. Pick up the body and use the index finger to push beak up. Remove beak and discard. Clean octopus thoroughly. Cut sac into 2 or 3 pieces. Place cleaned octopus in a shallow dish.

PAPPARDELLE WITH RABBIT AND PEPPER

Preparation time: 20 minutes
Total cooking time: 1 hour 50 minutes
Serves 4

1/4 cup olive oil
1 rabbit, jointed (about 2 lb)
2 slices Canadian bacon,
   cut into strips
1 onion, sliced
2 stalks celery, chopped
1 clove garlic, crushed
2 tablespoons all-purpose flour
1 teaspoon dried marjoram
16 oz can crushed tomatoes
1/2 cup red wine
1/2 cup water
1/4 cup tomato paste
salt and freshly ground black
   pepper to taste
1 pepper, seeded and sliced
1 eggplant, quartered and sliced
1 lb pappardelle
2 tablespoons freshly grated
   Parmesan cheese, for serving

➤ HEAT OIL in a large frying pan. Add the rabbit, brown well on all sides.

1 Transfer rabbit to a plate. Add bacon, onion, celery and garlic to the same pan. Stir over low heat until onion is soft.

2 Stir in flour and marjoram. Cook for 1 minute. Add undrained, crushed tomatoes, wine, water, tomato paste, salt and pepper; stir to combine.

3 Bring to boil, stirring constantly. Reduce heat and return rabbit to pan. Simmer, covered, for 1 1/2 hours or until rabbit is very tender, adding more water as required. Remove rabbit from sauce. Allow to cool slightly. Remove flesh from bones, and discard the bones.

4 Return rabbit flesh to sauce with pepper and eggplant. Simmer for another 15–20 minutes. About 15 minutes before sauce is ready, add papperdelle to a large pan of rapidly boiling water, cook until just tender. Drain well. Serve hot sauce over pasta. Sprinkle with a little Parmesan.

COOK'S FILE

Hint: Serve with crisp salad greens or lightly steamed carrots, zucchini, beans or broccoli.

SPAGHETTI PIZZAIOLA

Preparation time: 15 minutes
Total cooking time: 30 minutes
Serves 4

2 tablespoons olive oil
2 cloves garlic, crushed
8 oz ground beef or veal
2 x 16 oz cans crushed tomatoes
1/2 cup red wine
1 tablespoon chopped capers
1/2 teaspoon dried marjoram

1/2 teaspoon dried basil
salt and freshly ground black
   pepper to taste
2 tablespoons chopped fresh
   parsley
1 lb spaghetti

➤ HEAT OIL in a medium pan. Add garlic and stir over low heat for 1 minute.

1 Add meat and brown well, breaking up with a fork as it cooks. Drain.

2 Add to pan the undrained, crushed tomatoes, wine, capers, marjoram, basil, salt and pepper. Bring to boil. Reduce heat and simmer, uncovered, for 20 minutes or until sauce is reduced by half. Add parsley to pan and stir to mix.

3 While sauce is cooking, add the spaghetti to a large pan of rapidly boiling water and cook until just tender. Drain well and return to pan. Add sauce to pan and toss until mixed well. Serve immediately.

COOK'S FILE

Hint: Sprinkle with Parmesan cheese.

HOMESTYLE MEATBALLS WITH FUSILLI

Preparation time: 25 minutes
Total cooking time: 35 minutes
Serves 4

1 onion
1 1/2 lb ground pork and veal
    or ground beef
1 cup fresh bread crumbs
1/4 cup freshly grated Parmesan
    cheese
2 tablespoons chopped fresh
    parsley
1 egg, beaten
1 clove garlic, crushed
rind and juice of 1/2 lemon
salt and freshly ground black
    pepper to taste
1/4 cup all-purpose flour,
    seasoned
2 tablespoons olive oil
1 lb fusilli or spiral pasta

Sauce
15 oz can tomato puree
1/2 cup beef stock
1/2 cup red wine
2 tablespoons chopped fresh
    basil
1 clove garlic, crushed
salt and freshly ground black
    pepper to taste

➤ PEEL ONION and chop very finely.
1 In a large bowl, combine meat, bread crumbs, Parmesan, onion, parsley, egg, garlic, lemon rind and juice, salt and pepper. Roll tablespoonsful of mixture into balls and roll balls in seasoned flour.
2 Place oil in a frying pan and fry meatballs until golden. Remove from pan, drain on paper towels. Remove excess fat and meat juices from pan.
To make Sauce: In the same pan, combine tomato puree, stock, wine, basil, garlic, salt and pepper. Bring to boil.
3 Reduce heat and return meatballs to pan. Allow to simmer for 10–15 minutes. While meatballs and sauce are cooking, add fusilli to a large pan of rapidly boiling water and cook until just tender. Drain well. Serve fusilli with meatballs and sauce over the top.

C O O K ' S   F I L E

Hint: If desired, add 1 sliced zucchini to sauce in step 2.

GNOCCHI WITH TOMATO SAUCE

Preparation time: 35 minutes
Total cooking time: 45–50 minutes
Serves 4

1 lb potatoes, peeled and
  chopped
2 cups all-purpose flour, sifted
1/4 cup grated Parmesan
2 tablespoons butter or
  margarine, melted
salt and freshly ground black
  pepper to taste
2 tablespoons freshly grated
  Parmesan cheese, extra, for
  serving

Tomato Sauce
2 lb tomatoes, peeled and
  chopped
2 cloves garlic, crushed
1/2 cup red wine
1/4 cup finely chopped fresh basil
salt and freshly ground black
  pepper to taste

➤ COOK POTATO in pan of boiling water for 15–20 minutes or until soft.
1 Drain potato and mash until smooth. Transfer to a bowl. Add flour, cheese, butter, salt and pepper. Using a flat-bladed knife, mix to a firm dough. Knead on lightly floured surface until smooth.
2 Roll heaped teaspoonfuls of dough into oval shapes. Indent one side

using the back of a fork. Cook in batches in a large pan of rapidly boiling water for 3–5 minutes each batch. Gnocchi will float when cooked. Drain well. Keep warm.
3 To make Tomato Sauce: In a pan, combine tomatoes, garlic, wine, basil, salt and pepper. Bring to boil. Reduce heat and simmer for 15–20 minutes or until sauce begins to thicken. Toss gnocchi with sauce. Serve in warmed pasta bowls. Sprinkle with grated Parmesan cheese.

COOK'S FILE

Hint: If you prefer a meaty sauce, brown 8 oz ground veal or beef in 1 tablespoon olive oil before adding Tomato Sauce ingredients.

RIGATONI WITH CHORIZO AND TOMATO

Preparation time: 15 minutes
Total cooking time: 20–25 minutes
Serves 4

1 onion
8 oz chorizo sausage
2 tablespoons olive oil
16 oz can crushed tomatoes
1/2 cup dry white wine
1/2–1 teaspoon chopped chili, optional

salt and freshly ground black pepper to taste
12 oz rigatoni
2 tablespoons chopped fresh parsley, for serving
2 tablespoons freshly grated Parmesan cheese, for serving

➤ PEEL ONION and slice.
1 Cut chorizo sausage into slices. Heat oil in a frying pan. Add onion and stir over low heat until tender.
2 Add sausage to pan; cook turning frequently, for 2–3 minutes. Add undrained, crushed tomatoes, wine, chili, salt and pepper; stir. Bring to boil and reduce heat; simmer 15–20 minutes.
3 While the sauce is cooking, add rigatoni to a large pan of rapidly boiling water; cook until just tender. Drain well and return to pan. Add sauce to hot pasta with half of combined parsley and Parmesan cheese. Toss well to combine. Serve sprinkled with remaining combined parsley and Parmesan cheese.

COOK'S FILE

Variation: Use a different hot sausage in place of chorizo.

ZITI WITH VEGETABLES AND SAUSAGE

Preparation time: 10 minutes
Total cooking time: 35 minutes
Serves 4

1 red pepper
1 green pepper
1 small eggplant, sliced
1/4 cup olive oil
1 onion, sliced
1 clove garlic, crushed
8 oz small sausage links, sliced
16 oz can crushed tomatoes
1/2 cup red wine
1/4 cup halved pitted black olives
1 tablespoon chopped fresh basil
1 tablespoon chopped fresh
   parsley
salt and freshly ground black
   pepper to taste
1 lb ziti
2 tablespoons freshly grated
   Parmesan cheese, for serving

➤ CUT BOTH peppers in half. Remove seeds and membrane.

1 Place peppers under a hot broiler. Cook until skin blackens and blisters. Cover with a damp dish towel. When cool, peel off skin. Chop and set aside.

2 Brush eggplant with a little oil. Broil until golden each side, brushing with more oil as required. Set aside.

3 Heat remaining oil in a frying pan. Add onion and garlic and stir over low heat until the onion is tender. Add the sausage and cook until well browned.

4 Stir in undrained, crushed tomatoes, wine, olives, basil, parsley, salt and pepper. Bring to the boil. Reduce heat and simmer for 15 minutes. Add vegetables and heat through. While sauce is cooking, add ziti to a large pan of rapidly boiling water until just tender. Drain well and return to pan. Toss vegetables and sauce through hot pasta. Sprinkle with Parmesan cheese before serving.

COOK'S FILE

Hint: Serve with crisp green salad and crusty bread.

Ziti is a wide tubular pasta that is excellent with this dish but you can substitute fettuccine or spaghetti if you prefer.

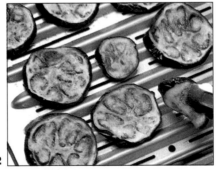

PASTA WITH BRAISED OXTAIL AND CELERY

Preparation time: 20 minutes
Total cooking time: 3 hours 45 minutes
Serves 4

3 lb oxtail, jointed
1/4 cup all-purpose flour, seasoned
1/4 cup olive oil
1 onion, finely chopped
2 cloves garlic, crushed
2 cups beef stock
16 oz can crushed tomatoes
1 cup dry white wine
6 whole cloves

2 bay leaves
salt and freshly ground black pepper to taste
3 stalks celery, finely chopped
1 lb penne
2 tablespoons butter or margarine
1/4 cup grated Parmesan

➤ PREHEAT OVEN to 325°F.
1 Dust oxtail in seasoned flour; shake off excess. Heat half the oil in a large pan. Brown oxtail over high heat, a few pieces at a time. Transfer to a large casserole dish.
2 Wipe pan clean with paper towels. Heat remaining oil in pan and add onion and garlic. Cook over low heat until onion is tender. Stir in stock, undrained, crushed tomatoes, wine, cloves, bay leaves, salt and pepper. Bring to boil. Pour over oxtail.
3 Bake, covered, for 2 1/2–3 hours. Add celery to dish. Bake, uncovered, for another 30 minutes. Towards the end of cooking time, add pasta to a large pan of rapidly boiling water and cook until tender. Drain well. Toss with butter and Parmesan. Serve oxtail and sauce with pasta.

COOK'S FILE

Hint: Seasoned flour is all-purpose flour to which seasonings of your choice have been added, for example, herbs, salt, pepper, dried mustard.

SPAGHETTI WITH SALAMI AND PEPPERS

Preparation time: 15 minutes
Total cooking time: 55 minutes
Serves 4–6

2 tablespoons olive oil
1 large onion, finely chopped
2 cloves garlic, crushed
5 oz spicy salami slices, cut into strips
2 large red peppers, chopped
28 oz can tomatoes
¹/₂ cup dry white wine
1 teaspoon dried basil
salt and pepper to taste
1 lb spaghetti

➤ HEAT OIL in a heavy-based frying pan.
1 Add onion, garlic and salami. Cook for 5 minutes, stirring, over medium heat. Add peppers; cover pan and cook for 5 minutes.
2 Add undrained, crushed tomatoes, wine and basil. Bring to boil and simmer, covered, for 15 minutes. Remove lid and cook for another 15 minutes or until the liquid is reduced and sauce is desired consistency. Add salt and pepper.
3 Add pasta to a large pan of rapidly boiling water and cook until just tender; drain and return to pan. Toss half the sauce with the pasta; divide between warmed serving dishes; top with remaining sauce and serve.

COOK'S FILE

Hints: Salami should be chosen according to your taste. Use less spicy salami if you prefer.
Sprinkle with grated fresh Parmesan.

PASTA SALADS

LINGUINE WITH BACON AND SESAME SEEDS

In a large salad bowl, combine 1 lb cooked, cooled linguine with 4 finely chopped slices of crisp fried bacon, 3 finely chopped hard-boiled eggs, $1/2$ cup freshly grated Parmesan cheese, $1/2$ cup chopped fresh parsley and $1/4$ cup toasted sesame seeds. Season to taste with salt and pepper, drizzle $1/4$ cup olive oil over the top and serve immediately. Garnish with fresh herbs, if desired. Serves 4–6.

Linguine with Bacon and Sesame Seeds

Spaghetti with Tomato and Olives

SPAGHETTI WITH TOMATO AND OLIVES

In a large salad bowl, combine 1 lb cooked, cooled spaghetti with 2 chopped tomatoes, 1 chopped red onion, $1/2$ cup olives and 1 cup fresh parsley leaves. Drizzle over dressing made by combining $1/4$ cup balsamic vinegar and $1/2$ cup olive oil, season to taste with salt and pepper. Serves 4–6.

PENNE WITH FAVA BEANS AND ARTICHOKES

In a large salad bowl, combine 1 lb cooked, cooled penne with 2 cups blanched, peeled fava beans, 4 chopped scallions, 6 quartered artichoke hearts, $1/2$ cup grated pecorino cheese and $1/4$ cup olive oil. Season to taste with salt and pepper. Garnish with fresh herbs, if desired. Serves 4–6.

FETTUCCINE WITH CHICKEN AND WALNUTS

In a large salad bowl, combine 1 lb cooked, cooled fettuccine with 2 cups cooked, shredded chicken, $1/2$ cup toasted walnuts, $1/2$ cup olives, 1 cup fresh basil leaves and $1/4$ cup lemon juice. Season to taste with salt and pepper; toss and serve immediately. Serves 4–6.

Penne with Fava Beans and Artichokes

Fettuccine with Chicken and Walnuts

Farfalle with
Tuna and Capers

Tagliatelle, Arugula and
Sundried Tomatoes

TAGLIATELLE, ARUGULA AND SUNDRIED TOMATOES

In a large salad bowl, combine 1 lb cooked, cooled tagliatelle with 3 cups arugula leaves, 10 chopped sundried tomatoes, 1 avocado, cut into slices, and a dressing of $1/2$ cup olive oil, $1/4$ cup white wine vinegar, and 1 tablespoon seeded mustard. Toss well, season to taste with salt and pepper. Serves 4–6.

MACARONI WITH SPINACH AND BACON

In a large salad bowl, combine 1 lb cooked macaroni, 2 cups shredded spinach, 4 slices crisp cooked bacon and a few slices of chopped prosciutto, 1 chopped red onion and $1/4$ cup freshly grated Parmesan. Drizzle $1/2$ cup olive oil over the top and season to taste with salt and pepper. Toss well and serve. Serves 4–6.

Spiral Pasta and
Artichokes

FARFALLE WITH TUNA AND CAPERS

In a large salad bowl, combine 1 lb cooked, cooled farfalle (butterfly pasta) with 13 oz can drained, flaked tuna, $6^{1}/2$ oz chopped mozzarella cheese, $1/2$ cup black olives, $1/2$ cup drained capers, fried in 1 tablespoon oil until very crisp, and $1/2$ cup chopped fresh basil. Toss well with $1/2$ cup lemon juice and season to taste with salt and pepper. Garnish with strips of lemon rind, if desired. Serves 4–6.

SPIRAL PASTA AND ARTICHOKES

Arrange some butter lettuce leaves on a platter, top with 1 lb cooked, cooled spiral pasta, 10 quartered artichoke hearts and 8 slices crisp cooked chopped pancetta. Toss with a dressing of 2 chopped cloves garlic, $1/4$ cup lemon juice, $1/2$ cup olive oil, and salt and pepper. Serves 4–6.

Macaroni with Spinach
and Bacon

59

CREAMY PASTA

TAGLIATELLE WITH ASPARAGUS AND HERBS

Preparation time: 15 minutes
Total cooking time: 15 minutes
Serves 4–6

1 lb tagliatelle
1 bunch asparagus
3 tablespoons butter
1 tablespoon chopped fresh
   parsley
1 tablespoon chopped fresh basil
1$\frac{1}{4}$ cups heavy cream
salt and pepper to taste
$\frac{1}{2}$ cup freshly grated Parmesan
   cheese

➤ COOK PASTA in a large pan of rapidly boiling water until just tender. Drain and return to pan.

1 While the pasta is cooking, cut asparagus spears into short pieces.
2 Heat butter in a medium pan, add the asparagus and stir over medium heat for 2 minutes or until just tender.
3 Add chopped parsley and basil, cream, salt and pepper. Cook for 2 minutes.
4 Add freshly grated Parmesan cheese to pan and stir well. When thoroughly mixed, add to warm pasta in pan and toss gently to distribute ingredients evenly. Serve in warmed pasta bowls.

COOK'S FILE

Hints: This dish looks attractive if you shave some extra Parmesan cheese and use it for garnish.

If desired, you can serve this dish as a first course for 8 people.

1

2

3

4

SPAGHETTI CARBONARA

Preparation time: 10 minutes
Total cooking time: 25 minutes
Serves 4–6

8 slices bacon
1 lb spaghetti
4 eggs
$^1/_2$ cup freshly grated Parmesan
   cheese
$1^1/_4$ cups heavy cream
freshly ground black pepper
   to taste

➤ CUT BACON into thin strips.
1 Add bacon strips to a heavy-based frying pan and cook over medium heat until crisp. Remove and drain on paper towels.
2 Add the pasta to a large pan of rapidly boiling water and cook until just tender. Drain in a colander and return to the pan. Set aside.
3 While the pasta is cooking, beat the eggs, Parmesan and cream in a small bowl. Add the cooked bacon to the bowl and pour the mixture over the hot pasta; toss well. Return the pan to heat and cook the mixture, over very

low heat, for $^1/_2$–1 minute, or until mixture just thickens. Add the pepper and serve immediately. May be garnished with sprigs of fresh herbs, if desired.

COOK'S FILE

Storage time: Best cooked just before serving.
Hint: Take care not to overcook sauce as it can curdle. Make sure the heat is very low after you have combined pasta with sauce. If you are using an electric burner you can turn the heat off at this stage.

FETTUCCINE ALFREDO

Preparation time: 10 minutes
Total cooking time: 15 minutes
Serves 4–6

1 lb fettuccine or tagliatelle
¹/₃ cup butter
1¹/₂ cups freshly grated
  Parmesan cheese

1¹/₄ cups heavy cream
¹/₄ cup chopped fresh parsley
salt and freshly ground black
  pepper to taste

➤ ADD PASTA to a large pan of rapidly boiling water and cook until just tender. Drain in a colander and return to pan.

1 While pasta is cooking, heat butter in a medium pan over low heat. Add

Parmesan and cream, bring to the boil, stirring regularly.

2 Add parsley, salt and pepper and stir to combine.

3 Add to pasta and toss well. Serve immediately.

COOK'S FILE

Hints: This dish will serve 8 as a first course.

Garnish with grated Parmesan.

PENNE WITH CREAMY TOMATO SAUCE

Preparation time: 25 minutes
Total cooking time: 20 minutes
Serves 4–6

2 slices bacon
4 large ripe tomatoes
1 lb penne
1 tablespoon olive oil
2 scallions, chopped
2 tablespoons chopped fresh
    basil
1¹/₄ cups heavy cream
salt and freshly ground black
    pepper to taste

➤ REMOVE AND DISCARD bacon rind. Cut bacon into small pieces.

1 Using a sharp knife, mark a small cross on the bottom of each tomato. Place tomatoes in boiling water for 1–2 minutes; plunge into cold water. Remove from water and peel skin down from cross.

2 Cut tomatoes in half and scoop out seeds with a teaspoon. Finely chop tomatoes. Add pasta to a large pan of rapidly boiling water and cook until just tender. Drain and keep warm.

3 While pasta is cooking, heat oil in a heavy-based frying pan. Cook bacon and scallions over medium heat, stirring occasionally, for 5 minutes. Add basil, cream, salt and pepper, and simmer for 5 minutes. Add tomatoes and cook for 2–3 minutes or until heated through. Divide pasta into warmed serving bowls. Top with sauce. Serve immediately.

COOK'S FILE

Storage time: If you like, you can prepare the tomatoes the day before cooking the dish and store in a sealed container in refrigerator.

1

2

3

SPAGHETTI WITH GORGONZOLA SAUCE

Preparation time: 10 minutes
Total cooking time: 20 minutes
Serves 4–6

12 oz spaghetti or bucatini
6¹/₂ oz gorgonzola cheese
2 tablespoons butter
1 stalk celery, finely chopped

1¹/₄ cups heavy cream
8 oz fresh ricotta cheese, beaten
   until smooth
freshly ground black pepper
   to taste

➤ ADD PASTA to a large pan of rapidly boiling water and cook until just tender. Drain and return to pan.
1 While pasta is cooking, chop gorgonzola cheese into small cubes.
2 Heat butter in a medium pan, add celery and stir for 2 minutes. Add cream, ricotta and gorgonzola cheeses; season to taste.
3 Bring to boil over low heat, stirring constantly, simmer 1 minute. Add sauce to pasta and toss well to combine.

COOK'S FILE

Hint: Garnish with chopped fresh parsley, if desired.
Note: Gorgonzola is a rich, strong Italian blue-veined cheese.

SHELLS WITH BROCCOLI AND ANCHOVY

Preparation time: 15 minutes
Total cooking time: 20 minutes
Serves 4–6

1 lb small shell pasta
1 lb broccoli
1 tablespoon oil
1 medium onion, chopped
1 clove garlic, crushed
3 anchovies, chopped
1¼ cups heavy cream
salt and freshly ground black
      pepper to taste

$\frac{1}{2}$ cup freshly grated Parmesan cheese, for serving

➤ ADD PASTA to a large pan of boiling water and cook until just tender. Drain and return to pan.

1 While pasta is cooking, cut broccoli into small florets. Cook broccoli in a pan of boiling water for 1 minute; drain. Place in cold water; drain again. Set aside.

2 Heat oil in a heavy-based frying pan. Add chopped onion, crushed garlic and chopped anchovies; cook over low heat, stirring, for 3 minutes.

3 Add cream to pan and, stirring constantly, bring to boil. Reduce heat and simmer for 2 minutes. Add broccoli florets and cook for 1 minute. Add salt and pepper. Add sauce to pasta and toss well to combine. Serve in warmed pasta plates. Sprinkle with freshly grated Parmesan cheese and serve immediately.

COOK'S FILE

Hints: When tossing sauce with the pasta, make sure all pieces of pasta are thoroughly coated with sauce. You can substitute different pastas such as macaroni or farfalle (butterfly pasta) if you prefer.
Variation: Use freshly grated pecorino cheese instead of Parmesan.

SPINACH FETTUCCINE WITH MUSHROOM SAUCE

Preparation time: 15 minutes
Total cooking time: 25 minutes
Serves 4–6

1 lb spinach or plain fettuccine
10 oz baby mushrooms
3 scallions
6 slices smoked ham or
      pancetta (1⅔ oz)
3 tablespoons butter
2 tablespoons chopped fresh
      parsley
1¼ cups heavy cream

salt and freshly ground black
      pepper to taste
2 tablespoons chopped fresh
      parsley, extra, for serving

➤ ADD PASTA to a large pan of rapidly boiling water and cook until just tender. Drain and return to pan.

1 While pasta is cooking, slice mushrooms finely. Trim scallions, removing dark green section; chop finely. Slice smoked ham or pancetta into thin strips.

2 Heat the butter in a medium pan, cook scallions and ham over medium heat for 3 minutes. Add mushrooms to the pan. Cover the pan and reduce heat; cook, stirring occasionally, for 5 minutes.

3 Add parsley, cream, salt and pepper. Simmer for 2 minutes. Add sauce to pasta, toss well to combine. Serve immediately in warmed pasta bowls. Sprinkle with extra parsley.

COOK'S FILE

Hints: Don't add all the pasta to the boiling water at once–add it gradually, making sure that the water continues to boil.

If spinach fettuccine is unavailable, you can use other varieties of pasta. Dried or fresh pasta are both delicious with this sauce.

Shells with Broccoli and Anchovy (top) and
Spinach Fettuccine with Mushroom Sauce

RIGATONI WITH SQUASH SAUCE

Preparation time: 15 minutes
Total cooking time: 25 minutes
Serves 4–6

2 lb winter squash
2 medium leeks
2 tablespoons butter
1/2 teaspoon ground nutmeg
1 lb rigatoni or large
   penne
1 1/4 cups heavy cream
1/4 cup water
1/4 cup toasted pine nuts

➤ PEEL SQUASH, discard seeds and cut squash into small cubes.

1 Remove and discard outer leaves and dark green section of leeks. Wash leeks thoroughly to remove all grit. Using a sharp knife, slice leeks finely.

2 Heat butter in large pan over low heat. Add sliced leek, cover pan, cook, stirring occasionally, for 5 minutes. Add squash and nutmeg, cover and cook for 8 minutes. While vegetables are cooking, add pasta to a large pan of boiling water and cook until just tender. Drain and keep warm.

3 Add cream and water to squash; bring sauce to boil. Cook, stirring occasionally, for 8 minutes or until squash is tender. Divide pasta between warmed serving bowls and top with sauce. Sprinkle with pine nuts and serve immediately.

COOK'S FILE

Hints: Butternut or acorn squash will give the sweetest flavor to this sauce.

To toast pine nuts, stir over low heat in a non-stick frying pan until lightly golden. Alternatively, spread on a baking sheet and bake at 350°F— be sure to check frequently as they brown quickly.

Variations: Add more nutmeg if you like a stronger flavor.

Use a smaller pasta, if preferred.

SPIRALS WITH FAVA BEAN SAUCE

Preparation time: 30 minutes
Total cooking time: 25 minutes
Serves 4–6

1 lb spiral pasta or penne
2 cups frozen fava beans
4 slices bacon
2 medium leeks
2 tablespoons olive oil
1¹/₄ cups heavy cream
2 teaspoons grated lemon rind
salt and freshly ground black
   pepper to taste

➤ ADD PASTA to a large pan of rapidly boiling water and cook until just tender. Drain and return to pan.

1 While the pasta is cooking, plunge fava beans into a medium pan of boiling water. Remove immediately and cool in cold water. Drain and allow to cool. Peel rough outside skin from beans.

2 Remove and discard rind from bacon. Chop bacon into small pieces. Remove and discard outer leaves and dark green section of leeks. Wash leeks thoroughly to remove all dirt and grit. Using a sharp knife, slice leeks finely.

3 Heat oil in heavy-based frying pan. Add leek and bacon and cook over medium heat, stirring occasionally, for 8 minutes or until leek is golden. Add cream and lemon rind; cook for 2 minutes. Add prepared fava beans, salt and pepper.

4 Add the sauce to pasta and toss well to combine. Serve immediately in warmed pasta bowls.

COOK'S FILE

Storage time: Fava beans can be cooked and peeled in advance and refrigerated in a covered container.

Hint: To peel fava beans, break the top off and squeeze beans out. Leaving the hard outside skin on the fava bean will change the delicate texture and flavor of this dish—it is worth the extra effort.

Fresh fava beans can be used instead of frozen. If they are very young, you can leave the skin on. Old beans must be peeled. Cook, after peeling, 15 minutes and add to dish.

1

2

3

4

SPAGHETTI WITH PRIMAVERA SAUCE

Preparation time: 25 minutes
Total cooking time: 15 minutes
Serves 4–6

1 lb spaghetti or fettuccine
1 bunch fresh asparagus
1 cup frozen fava beans
2 tablespoons butter
1 stalk celery, sliced
1 cup frozen green peas
1¹/₄ cups heavy cream
¹/₂ cup freshly grated Parmesan

salt and freshly ground black pepper to taste

➤ ADD PASTA to a pan of rapidly boiling water and cook until just tender. Drain and return to pan.

1 While pasta is cooking, cut asparagus into small pieces. Bring a medium pan of water to boil, add asparagus, cook 2 minutes. Using a slotted spoon, remove from the pan and plunge in cold water.

2 Plunge the fava beans into a medium pan of boiling water. Remove them immediately and cool in cold water. Drain and allow to cool. Peel the rough outside skin from the fava beans.

3 Heat the butter in a heavy-based frying pan. Add celery and stir for 2 minutes. Add peas and cream; cook for 3 minutes. Add asparagus, fava beans, Parmesan, salt and pepper and bring sauce to boil; cook for 1 minute. Add the sauce to spaghetti and toss to combine. Serve immediately in warmed pasta bowls.

COOK'S FILE

Variation: Use different vegetables such as leeks, zucchini and sugar peas with fresh chopped dill or basil.

SPAGHETTI WITH CREAMY GARLIC MUSSELS

Preparation time: 20 minutes
Total cooking time: 12 minutes
Serves 4

1 lb spaghetti
3 lb mussels in the shell
2 tablespoons olive oil
2 cloves garlic, crushed

¹/₂ cup white wine
1 cup heavy cream
2 tablespoons chopped fresh basil
salt and freshly ground black pepper to taste

➤ ADD SPAGHETTI to a large pan of rapidly boiling water and cook until just tender. Drain and keep warm.

1 While the spaghetti is cooking, remove the beards from the mussels and wash away any grit. Set aside.

Heat the oil in a large pan. Add the garlic and stir over low heat for 30 seconds.

2 Add the wine and the mussels. Simmer, covered, for 5 minutes. Remove mussels and set aside.

3 Add the cream, basil, salt and pepper to pan. Simmer for 2 minutes, stirring occasionally. Serve sauce and mussels over spaghetti.

COOK'S FILE

Hint: Serve with crusty bread.

CREAMY SHRIMP WITH FETTUCCINE

Preparation time: 20 minutes
Total cooking time: 15 minutes
Serves 4

1 lb fettuccine
1 lb raw shrimp
2 tablespoons butter
1 tablespoon olive oil
6 scallions, chopped
1 clove garlic, crushed
1 cup heavy cream
salt and freshly ground black
    pepper to taste
2 tablespoons chopped fresh
    parsley, for serving

➤ ADD FETTUCCINE to a large pan of rapidly boiling water and cook until just tender. Drain well and return to the pan.

1 While fettuccine is cooking, peel and devein shrimp.

2 Heat butter and oil in a frying pan. Add scallions and garlic and stir over low heat 1 minute. Add shrimp. Cook for 2–3 minutes or until flesh changes color. Remove shrimp from pan and set aside. Add cream to pan and bring to boil. Reduce heat and simmer until sauce begins to thicken. Return shrimp to pan and add salt and pepper. Simmer for 1 minute.

3 Add shrimp and sauce to fettuccine and toss. Serve in warmed pasta bowls. Sprinkle with parsley.

COOK'S FILE

Variations: In step 1, add 1 red pepper, seeded and sliced, and 1 leek, dark green section removed and white part cleaned thoroughly and sliced very finely.

Use scallops instead of shrimp or a mixture of both.

FARFALLE WITH TUNA, MUSHROOMS AND CREAM

Preparation time: 10 minutes
Total cooking time: 15 minutes
Serves 4

$^{1}/_{4}$ cup butter or margarine
1 tablespoon olive oil
1 onion, chopped
1 clove garlic, crushed
4 oz mushrooms, sliced
1 cup heavy cream
2 x 7 oz cans tuna, drained, flaked

1 tablespoon lemon juice
1 tablespoon chopped fresh
    parsley
salt and freshly ground black
    pepper to taste
1 lb farfalle (butterfly pasta)

➤ HEAT BUTTER and oil in large frying pan. Add the onion and garlic; stir over low heat until the onion is tender.

1 Add mushrooms to pan. Cook for 2 minutes. Pour in cream. Bring to boil. Reduce heat. Simmer until sauce begins to thicken.

2 Add flaked tuna, lemon juice, pars-

ley, salt and pepper to cream mixture; stir to combine. Heat gently, stirring constantly.

3 While the sauce is cooking, add the farfalle to a large pan of rapidly boiling water and cook until just tender. Drain well and return to the pan. Add the sauce to the farfalle and toss to combine. Serve in warmed pasta bowls.

COOK'S FILE

Hint: Serve with a fresh green salad or steamed vegetables.

Variation: Use canned salmon, drained and flaked, instead of tuna.

FETTUCCINE WITH SMOKED SALMON

Preparation time: 10 minutes
Total cooking time: 10 minutes
Serves 4

3¹/₃ oz smoked salmon
¹/₄ cup sundried tomatoes
1 tablespoon olive oil
1 clove garlic, crushed
1 cup heavy cream
¹/₄ cup snipped fresh chives
¹/₄ teaspoon mustard powder

salt and freshly ground black
 pepper to taste
2 teaspoons lemon juice
12 oz fettuccine
2 tablespoons freshly grated
 Parmesan, for serving
snipped fresh chives, extra, for
 serving

➤ SLICE SMOKED salmon into pieces.
1 Chop the sundried tomatoes. Heat oil in a frying pan. Add garlic and stir over low heat for 30 seconds. Add cream, chives, mustard powder, salt and pepper; bring to boil. Reduce heat

and simmer, stirring, until sauce begins to thicken.
2 Add salmon and lemon juice; stir to combine. Heat gently. While sauce is cooking, add pasta to large pan of rapidly boiling water; cook until just tender. Drain well and return to pan.
3 Toss the sauce through the hot pasta. Serve immediately topped with sundried tomatoes, Parmesan and chives.

COOK'S FILE

Hint: Grow your own chives in the garden or in pots.

FETTUCCINE WITH CAVIAR

Preparation time: 15 minutes
Total cooking time: 15 minutes
Serves 4

2 hard-boiled eggs
4 scallions
1 cup light sour cream
1²/₃ oz red caviar
2 tablespoons chopped fresh dill

1 tablespoon lemon juice
freshly ground black pepper to
    taste
1 lb fettuccine

➤ PEEL EGGS and chop into small
pieces. Trim scallions, discarding dark
green tops; chop finely.
1 In a small bowl place sour cream,
eggs, scallions, caviar, dill, lemon juice
and pepper. Mix ingredients well and
set aside.
2 Add fettuccine to a large pan of

rapidly boiling water and cook until
just tender. Drain well; return to pan.
3 Toss caviar mixture through hot
pasta. Serve garnished with a sprig of
fresh dill, if desired.

COOK'S FILE

Note: Use large red roe, not small
supermarket variety.
Hint: To hard-boil an egg, place cold
egg in cold water. Bring water to boil,
simmer 5–6 minutes. Cool under cold
running water.

1

2

3

PENNE WITH CHICKEN AND MUSHROOMS

Preparation time: 15 minutes
Total cooking time: 25 minutes
Serves 4

2 tablespoons butter
1 tablespoon olive oil
1 onion, sliced
1 clove garlic, crushed
2 oz prosciutto, chopped
8 oz chicken thigh fillets,
    trimmed and sliced
4 oz mushrooms, sliced
1 tomato, peeled, halved and
    sliced

1 tablespoon tomato paste
1/2 cup white wine
1 cup heavy cream
salt and freshly ground black
    pepper to taste
1 lb penne
2 tablespoons freshly grated
    Parmesan cheese, for serving

➤ HEAT BUTTER and oil in a large frying pan.

1 Add onion and garlic and stir over low heat until onion is tender. Add prosciutto to pan and fry until crisp.

2 Add the chicken and cook over medium heat for 3 minutes. Add mushrooms and cook for another 2 minutes. Add tomato and tomato paste and stir until combined. Add wine and stir. Bring to boil. Reduce heat and simmer until liquid is reduced by half.

3 Stir in cream, salt and pepper. Bring to boil. Reduce heat and simmer until sauce begins to thicken. While sauce is cooking, add penne to a large pan of rapidly boiling water and cook until just tender. Drain well and return to pan. Add sauce to pasta and toss to combine. Serve immediately, sprinkled with Parmesan.

COOK'S FILE

Hint: If you prefer, you can use ground chicken in this recipe instead of sliced chicken fillets.

RIGATONI WITH SAUSAGE AND PARMESAN

Preparation time: 10 minutes
Total cooking time: 15 minutes
Serves 4

2 oz mushrooms, sliced
1 lb Italian pork sausage links
    or salami
2 tablespoons olive oil
1 onion, sliced
1 clove garlic, crushed
1/2 cup dry white wine
1 lb rigatoni

1 cup heavy cream
2 eggs
1/2 cup freshly grated Parmesan
    cheese
2 tablespoons chopped fresh
    parsley
salt and freshly ground black
    pepper to taste

➤ SLICE MUSHROOMS finely.

1 Cut sausage into chunks. Heat oil in a large frying pan.

2 Add the onion and garlic and stir over low heat until onion is tender. Add sausage and mushrooms. Cook until sausage is cooked through. Add the wine and bring mixture to boil. Reduce heat; simmer until reduced by half.

3 While sauce is cooking, add rigatoni to a large pan of rapidly boiling water; cook until just tender. Drain well; return to pan. In large jug, whisk together cream, eggs, 1/4 cup of the Parmesan, parsley, salt and pepper. Add to rigatoni; add sausage mixture; toss. Serve sprinkled with remaining Parmesan cheese.

COOK'S FILE

Hint: You can freeze leftover wine for use in recipes such as this one.

*Penne with Chicken and Mushrooms (top) and
Rigatoni with Sausage and Parmesan*

TAGLIATELLE WITH CHICKEN LIVERS AND CREAM

Preparation time: 20 minutes
Total cooking time: 15 minutes
Serves 4

1 onion
10 oz chicken livers
2 tablespoons olive oil
1 clove garlic, crushed
1 cup heavy cream
1 tablespoon snipped chives
1 teaspoon seeded mustard

salt and freshly ground black
   pepper to taste
2 eggs, beaten
12 oz tagliatelle
2 tablespoons freshly grated
   Parmesan cheese, for serving
snipped chives, for serving

➤ PEEL ONION and chop finely.
1 Trim chicken livers and chop them into small pieces.
2 Heat oil in a large frying pan. Add onion and garlic and stir over low heat until onion is tender. Add chicken livers to pan. Cook gently for 2–3 minutes. Remove from heat. Stir cream, chives, mustard, salt and pepper into chicken livers. Return to heat. Bring to boil.
3 Add beaten eggs; stir quickly to combine. Remove from heat. While sauce is cooking, add tagliatelle to a large pan of rapidly boiling water and cook until just tender. Drain well and return to pan. Add the sauce to the hot pasta and toss well to combine. Serve in warmed pasta bowls. Sprinkle with Parmesan cheese and snipped chives.

COOK'S FILE

Hint: Snip chives with kitchen scissors.

LINGUINE WITH LEMON CREAMY SAUCE

Preparation time: 10 minutes
Total cooking time: 20 minutes
Serves 4

13 oz fresh linguine or spaghetti
1¼ cups heavy cream
1 cup chicken stock
1 tablespoon grated lemon rind

salt and pepper to taste
¼ teaspoon saffron threads or powder, optional

➤ ADD PASTA to a large pan of rapidly boiling water until just tender. Drain and keep warm.

1 While pasta is cooking, combine cream, chicken stock and lemon rind in a large frying pan. Bring to boil, stirring occasionally.

2 Reduce heat and simmer for 10 minutes. Season to taste with salt and pepper. Add cooked pasta and cook for another 2–3 minutes.

3 Sprinkle with saffron threads; stir and serve immediately. Garnish with fine strips of lemon rind, if desired.

COOK'S FILE

Hint: Saffron is available from supermarkets and specialty food shops. If saffron is unavailable, use ¼ teaspoon turmeric.

1

2

3

SEMOLINA GNOCCHI BAKED WITH CHEESE

Preheat oven to moderate 350°F and grease a 6-cup oven-proof dish. Bring 4 cups milk to the boil in a medium pan. Slowly sprinkle 8 oz fine semolina over the surface of the milk, whisking to prevent lumps. Cook for 5–8 minutes stirring constantly until mixture forms a smooth thick ball. Stir in 2 egg yolks, $1/2$ cup freshly grated Parmesan cheese, $1/2$ cup melted butter and season to taste with salt and pepper. Lightly dampen counter top with water, spread semolina mixture onto surface with a wet flat-bladed knife. Smooth out mixture to about $1/2$ inch thick. Cut into rounds with a wet $2^1/2$ inch cutter. Place half of gnocchi rounds in the base of the dish; pour over $2/3$ cup tomato puree and place remaining gnocchi rounds over the top. Sprinkle with $1/2$ cup freshly grated Parmesan cheese and dot with butter. Bake 20–25 minutes or until crisp and golden brown. Garnish with fresh basil leaves. Serves 4–6.

Spinach and Ricotta Gnocchi

Semolina Gnocchi Baked with Cheese

GNOCCHI

SPINACH AND RICOTTA GNOCCHI

Place 4 slices crustless white bread in a shallow dish. Cover with $1/2$ cup milk and allow to stand for 10 minutes. Squeeze out excess liquid. Thaw 1 lb frozen spinach and squeeze out all excess liquid. Place bread, spinach, 8 oz ricotta cheese, 3 eggs, $1/2$ cup freshly grated Parmesan cheese, $1/2$ teaspoon nutmeg and salt and pepper to taste, in a food processor. Process for 20 seconds or until combined. Refrigerate for 1 hour. Lightly coat fingertips in flour and roll rounded teaspoonfuls of mixture into little flat dumplings. Bring a medium pan of water to a gentle boil, cook 5 gnocchi at a time for about 2 minutes or until they float, remove with a slotted spoon to warmed serving plates. Serve immediately, drizzled with foaming butter. Garnish with shaved Parmesan cheese and sage leaves, if desired. Serves 4–6 .

NOTE: Spinach gnocchi is very soft and must be handled gently—not over-handled or it will toughen and break up.

DRY-ROASTED BUTTERNUT GNOCCHI WITH NUTMEG

Preheat oven to moderate 350°F. Cut 3 lb butternut squash into large wedges, place in a baking dish and cook for 1 hour or until tender. Cool and peel. Process in a food processor until smooth. Remove to a large mixing bowl. Stir in 2 cups all-purpose flour, 2 tablespoons freshly grated Parmesan cheese and 1 egg. Cover with plastic wrap and refrigerate 1¹/₂ hours. Fit a large piping bag with a star nozzle and fill with mixture. Hold the piping bag over the boiling water; squeeze the mixture out and cut into lengths using scissors, letting gnocchi fall straight into the water. Cook in 4 batches in boiling water for about 4 minutes or until they float. Remove with a slotted spoon to warmed serving dishes. Serve immediately with foaming butter, sprinkled with freshly ground nutmeg. Garnish with sprigs of fresh oregano, if desired. Serves 4–6.

Potato Gnocchi with Tomato and Basil Sauce

Dry-roasted Butternut Gnocchi with Nutmeg

POTATO GNOCCHI WITH TOMATO AND BASIL SAUCE

Heat 1 tablespoon oil in a frying pan. Add 1 chopped onion, 1 stalk chopped celery and 2 chopped carrots. Cook for 5 minutes, stirring regularly. Add a 28 oz can crushed tomatoes with liquid, 1 teaspoon sugar and salt and pepper to taste. Bring to boil, reduce heat and simmer over very low heat 20 minutes. Process until smooth in a food processor; add ¹/₂ cup chopped fresh basil leaves. Set aside. Peel and chop 2 lb old potatoes; cook 15 minutes in boiling water until very tender. Drain and mash until smooth. Stir in 2 tablespoons butter and 2 cups all-purpose flour. Beat in 2 eggs. Cool. Turn potato mixture onto a floured surface, divide into 2, roll each batch into long sausages. Cut into 1–1¹/₂ inch pieces and roll each piece along the outside of a fork to give a traditional pattern. Cook gnocchi in 4 batches in boiling water for about 3 minutes or until they float. Drain with a slotted spoon to warmed serving plates. Serve with tomato sauce and freshly grated Parmesan cheese. Serves 4–6.

NOTE: Gnocchi must not be handled more than necessary or overcooked or it becomes tough. Keep all ingredients chilled and the kitchen cool.

Gnocchi can be made and formed into desired shapes before freezing in between freezer paper in an airtight container. It will keep for up to 2 months. When you wish to use it, cook frozen (do not defrost) in boiling water, adding 30 seconds extra cooking time if necessary.

BAKED & FILLED

BASIL TORTELLINI WITH BACON AND TOMATO SAUCE

Preparation: 15 minutes
Total cooking time: 25 minutes
Serves 4

1 lb fresh or dried basil
    tortellini or orecchiette
1 tablespoon olive oil
4 slices bacon, chopped
2 cloves garlic, crushed
1 medium onion, chopped
1 teaspoon chopped fresh
    chilies
16 oz can tomatoes
1/2 cup heavy cream
2 tablespoons chopped
    fresh basil

➤ COOK PASTA in a pan of rapidly boiling water until just tender. Drain and return to pan.

1 While pasta is cooking, heat oil in a medium heavy-based pan. Add bacon, garlic and onion and cook 5 minutes over medium heat stirring regularly.

2 Add chili and undrained, chopped tomatoes; reduce heat and simmer, uncovered, for 10 minutes.

3 Add cream and basil; cook for 1 minute.

4 Add sauce to pasta and toss well. Serve immediately.

COOK'S FILE

Storage time: This dish can be made up to the end of step 2, one day in advance.

Variation: Use a meat or cheese-filled pasta.

CHICKEN RAVIOLI WITH BUTTERED SAGE SAUCE

Preparation time: 15 minutes
Total cooking time: 10 minutes
Serves 4

1 lb fresh or dried chicken-filled
    ravioli or agnolotti
1/4 cup butter
4 scallions, chopped

2 tablespoons fresh sage,
    chopped
salt and pepper to taste
1/2 cup freshly grated Parmesan
    cheese, for serving
fresh sage leaves, extra, for
    garnish

➤ ADD RAVIOLI to a large pan of rapidly boiling water.

1 Cook ravioli until just tender. Drain pasta in colander and return to pan.

2 While ravioli is cooking, melt butter in a heavy-based pan. Add the scallions and sage and stir for 2 minutes. Add salt and pepper.

3 Add sauce to pasta; toss well. Pour into a warmed serving platter and sprinkle with Parmesan. Garnish with fresh sage leaves; serve immediately.

COOK'S FILE

Hint: Bite through a piece of ravioli to test whether it is done.

CHEESE TORTELLINI WITH NUTTY HERB SAUCE

Preparation time: 15 minutes
Total cooking time: 10 minutes
Serves 4–6

1 lb ham and cheese-filled fresh
  or dried tortellini or ravioli
3$^{1}/_{3}$ oz walnuts
$^{1}/_{4}$ cup butter

3$^{1}/_{3}$ oz pine nuts
2 tablespoons chopped fresh
  parsley
2 teaspoons fresh thyme
salt and freshly ground black
  pepper to taste
$^{1}/_{4}$ cup fresh ricotta cheese
$^{1}/_{4}$ cup heavy cream

➤ ADD PASTA to a pan of rapidly boiling water and cook until just tender. Drain and return to pan.
1 Chop walnuts into small pieces.

While pasta is cooking, heat butter in heavy-based pan over medium heat until foaming.
2 Add walnuts and pine nuts and stir for 5 minutes or until golden brown. Add parsley, thyme, salt and pepper.
3 Beat ricotta with cream. Add Nutty Herb Sauce to pasta and toss well to combine. Top with a dollop of ricotta cream. Serve immediately.

COOK'S FILE

Variation: Use chopped hazelnuts.

CANNELLONI

Preparation time: 35 minutes
Total cooking time: 1 hour 10 minutes
Serves 4–6

Beef and Spinach Filling
1 tablespoon olive oil
1 onion, chopped
1 clove garlic, crushed
1 lb ground beef
8 oz package frozen spinach, thawed
1/4 cup tomato paste
1/2 cup ricotta cheese
1 egg
1/2 teaspoon ground oregano
salt and freshly ground black pepper to taste

Béchamel Sauce
1 cup milk
1 sprig fresh parsley
5 peppercorns
2 tablespoons butter
1 tablespoon all-purpose flour
1/2 cup heavy cream
salt to taste
freshly ground black pepper to taste

Tomato Sauce
15 oz can tomato puree
2 tablespoons chopped fresh basil
1 clove garlic, crushed
1/2 teaspoon sugar
salt to taste
freshly ground black pepper, to taste

12–15 instant cannelloni tubes
1 cup freshly grated mozzarella cheese
1/2 cup freshly grated Parmesan cheese

➤ PREHEAT OVEN to moderate 350°F. Lightly oil a large shallow casserole dish. Set aside.

1 To make Beef and Spinach Filling: Heat oil in a frying pan. Add onion and garlic and stir over low heat until onion is tender. Add beef and brown well, breaking up with a spoon or fork as it cooks. Drain. Add spinach and tomato paste. Cook, stirring, for 1 minute. Remove from heat. In a small bowl, mix ricotta, egg, oregano, salt and pepper. Add to beef mixture; stir to combine. Set aside.

2 To make Béchamel Sauce: Place milk, parsley and peppercorns in a small pan. Bring to boil. Remove from heat. Allow to stand for 10 minutes. Strain, discard flavorings. Melt butter in a small pan. Add flour. Cook, stirring, for 1 minute. Remove from heat. Gradually blend in strained milk, stirring until mixture is smooth. Return to heat. Cook, stirring constantly over medium heat, until sauce boils and thickens. Reduce heat and simmer for 3 minutes. Add cream, salt and pepper; stir.

3 To make Tomato Sauce: Place all ingredients in medium pan; stir to combine. Bring to boil. Reduce heat. Simmer for 5 minutes.

4 Spoon Beef and Spinach Filling into a piping bag and fill cannelloni tubes or fill using a teaspoon.

5 Spoon a little of the Tomato Sauce in the base of the prepared casserole dish. Arrange cannelloni on top.

6 Pour Béchamel Sauce over cannelloni followed by the remaining tomato sauce. Sprinkle combined cheeses over the top. Bake, uncovered, for 30–35 minutes or until golden.

COOK'S FILE

Hint: Serve with a mixed green salad or steam some vegetables such as broccoli or beans, if desired.

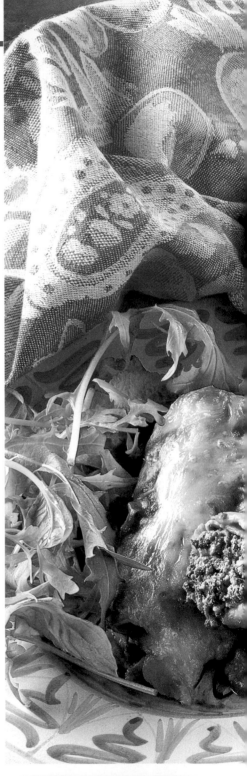

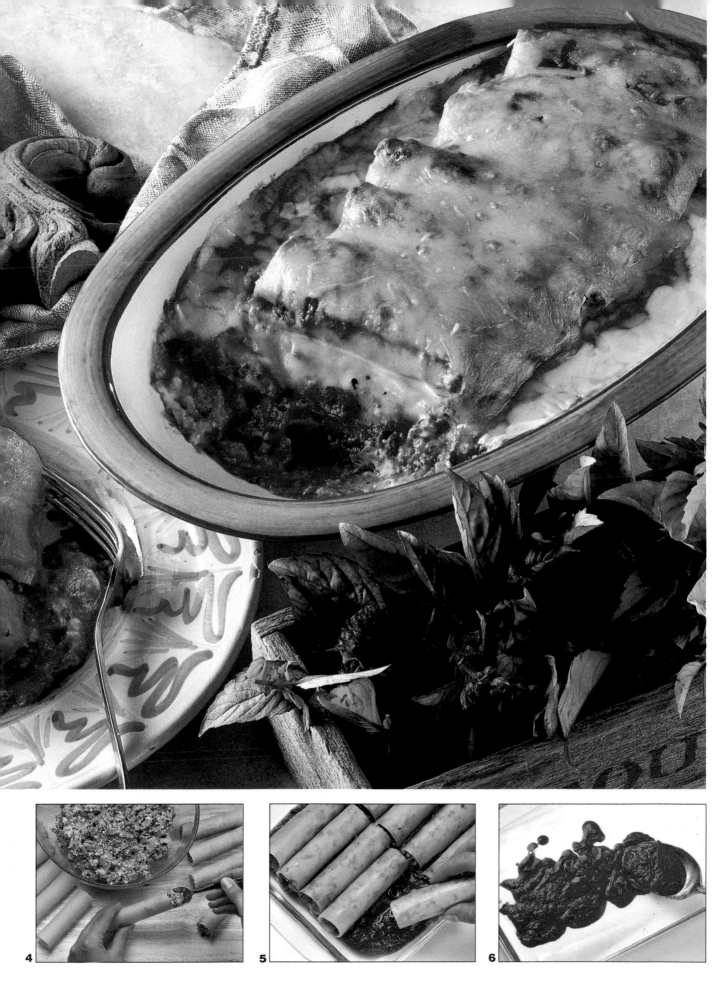

BAKED SPAGHETTI FRITTATA

Preparation time: 15 minutes
Total cooking time: 35 minutes
Serves 4

2 tablespoons butter
4 oz mushrooms, sliced
1 green pepper, seeded and
    chopped
4 oz ham, sliced
1/2 cup frozen peas

6 eggs
1 cup light cream or milk
salt and pepper to taste
4 oz spaghetti, cooked and
    chopped
2 tablespoons chopped fresh
    parsley
1/4 cup freshly grated Parmesan
    cheese

➤ PREHEAT OVEN to moderate 350°F. Grease a 9 inch flan dish.
1 Melt the butter in a frying pan. Add the mushrooms; cook over low heat

for 2–3 minutes.
2 Add pepper; cook 1 minute. Stir in ham and peas. Remove pan from heat; allow mixture to cool slightly.
3 In a small bowl, whisk eggs, cream, salt and pepper. Add spaghetti, parsley and mushroom mixture to bowl and stir. Pour into prepared dish and sprinkle with Parmesan cheese. Bake for 25–30 minutes.

COOK'S FILE

Hint: Serve with char-grilled vegetables and leafy salad greens.

BAKED SEAFOOD AND PASTA

Preparation time: 15 minutes
Total cooking time: 45 minutes
Serves 4–6

8 oz package no-cook lasagna
   sheets
1 lb boneless fish fillets
4 oz scallops, cleaned
1 lb raw shrimp, shelled
   and deveined
$^1/_2$ cup butter or margarine
1 leek, cleaned and sliced
$^2/_3$ cup all-purpose flour
2 cups milk
2 cups dry white wine
1 cup freshly grated cheddar
   cheese
salt to taste
freshly ground black pepper
   to taste

$^1/_2$ cup heavy cream
$^1/_2$ cup freshly grated Parmesan
   cheese
2 tablespoons chopped fresh
   parsley

➤ PREHEAT OVEN to moderate
350°F. Line a greased shallow lasagna
dish (approximately 12 x 12 inches)
with lasagna sheets, breaking them to
fill any gaps. Set aside.
1 Chop fish and scallops into even-
sized pieces. Chop shrimp.
2 Melt butter in large pan. Add leek
and cook, stirring, 1 minute. Add flour
and cook, stirring, 1 minute. Gradually
blend in milk and wine, stirring until
mixture is smooth. Cook, stirring
constantly, over medium heat until
sauce boils and thickens. Reduce heat;
simmer 3 minutes. Remove from heat;
stir in cheese, salt and pepper. Add
seafood; simmer 1 minute. Remove
from heat.

3 Spoon half the seafood mixture
over lasagna sheets. Top with a layer
of lasagna sheets. Continue layering,
finishing with lasagna sheets.
4 Pour cream over the top. Sprinkle
with combined Parmesan and parsley.
Bake, uncovered, for 30 minutes or
until bubbling and golden.

COOK'S FILE

Note: No-cook lasagna is available in
straight or ridged sheets.

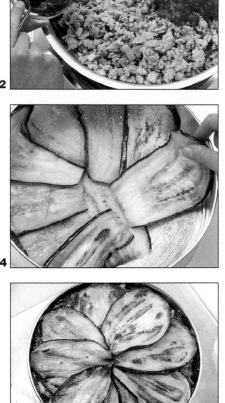

MACARONI EGGPLANT CAKE

Preparation time: 30 minutes
Total cooking time: 1 hour
Serves 4–6

4 oz macaroni
2–3 eggplant, sliced thinly lengthwise
salt
olive oil
1 onion, chopped
1 clove garlic, crushed
1 lb ground pork, beef or chicken
16 oz can crushed tomatoes
2 tablespoons tomato paste
salt and freshly ground black pepper to taste
1/2 cup frozen peas
1 cup freshly grated mozzarella cheese
1/2 cup freshly grated cheddar cheese
1 egg, beaten
1/2 cup freshly grated Parmesan cheese

➤ GREASE AND LINE a deep 9 inch round springform pan. Add macaroni to a large pan of rapidly boiling water and cook until just tender. Drain and set aside.

1 Arrange the eggplant on trays. Sprinkle with salt. Allow to stand for 20 minutes. Rinse well. Pat dry with paper towels. Heat 2 tablespoons oil in a frying pan. Cook eggplant in batches in a single layer until golden on each side. Add more oil as required. Drain on paper towels.

2 Add onion and crushed garlic to same pan and stir over low heat until onion is tender. Add meat and brown, breaking up any lumps with a spoon or fork as it cooks. Drain. Add undrained, crushed tomatoes, tomato paste, salt and pepper and stir well. Bring to boil. Reduce heat and simmer for 15–20 minutes. Set aside.

3 In a bowl, place peas, macaroni, mozzarella and cheddar cheeses, egg and half the Parmesan. Use a wooden spoon to mix. Set aside.

4 Preheat oven to moderate 350°F.

Place a slice of eggplant in the center on the base of prepared pan. Arrange three-quarters of remaining eggplant in an overlapping pattern to completely cover the base and sides of pan. Sprinkle with half the remaining Parmesan cheese.

5 Combine the meat mixture with macaroni mixture. Carefully spoon filling into eggplant case, packing down well. Arrange remaining eggplant slices, overlapping, over the filling. Sprinkle with the remaining Parmesan cheese.

6 Bake, uncovered, 25–30 minutes or until golden. Allow to rest for 5 minutes before unmolding onto a serving plate. Serve with salad, if desired.

COOK'S FILE

Variations: If preferred, omit the ground meat and add chopped cooked Italian sausage and chopped cooked chicken to the tomato mixture.

Serve with some extra tomato sauce made by simmering undrained, crushed tomatoes with a little garlic, pepper and chopped basil until thickened.

CONCHIGLIE WITH CHICKEN AND RICOTTA

Preparation time: 15 minutes
Total cooking time: 1 hour 10 minutes
Serves 4

1 lb conchiglie (shell pasta)
2 tablespoons olive oil
1 onion, chopped
1 clove garlic, crushed
2 oz prosciutto, sliced
4 oz mushrooms, chopped
8 oz ground chicken
2 tablespoons tomato paste
16 oz can crushed tomatoes
1/2 cup dry white wine
1 teaspoon dried oregano
salt and freshly ground black
   pepper to taste
8 oz ricotta cheese
1 cup grated mozzarella

1 teaspoon snipped fresh chives
1 tablespoon chopped fresh
   parsley
1/4 cup freshly grated Parmesan
   cheese

➤ ADD CONCHIGLIE TO a large pan of rapidly boiling water and cook until just tender. Drain well.

1 Heat oil in a large frying pan. Add onion and garlic and stir over low heat until onion is tender. Add prosciutto and stir for 1 minute.

2 Add mushrooms to pan and cook for 2 minutes. Add ground chicken. Brown well, breaking up with a fork as it cooks.

3 Stir in tomato paste, undrained, crushed tomatoes, wine, oregano, salt and pepper. Bring to boil. Reduce heat. Simmer for 20 minutes.

4 Preheat oven to moderate 350°F. Combine ricotta, mozzarella, chives, parsley and half the Parmesan cheese. Spoon a little of the mixture into each shell. Spoon some of the chicken sauce into the base of a casserole dish. Arrange conchiglie on top. Spread remaining sauce over the top. Sprinkle with remaining Parmesan cheese. Bake 25–30 minutes or until golden.

COOK'S FILE

Note: Shell pastas vary in size—medium or large shells are best for this dish.

VEAL TORTELLINI WITH CREAMY SPINACH SAUCE

Preparation time: 15 minutes
Total cooking time: 20 minutes
Serves 4

1 lb fresh or dried veal-filled
    tortellini
10 oz package frozen spinach
1/4 cup butter
1 medium onion, chopped
1 clove garlic, crushed

1/2 teaspoon nutmeg
1 1/4 cups heavy cream
1/2 cup light chicken stock
salt and freshly ground black
    pepper to taste
1/4 cup grated pecorino cheese,
    for serving

➤ ADD PASTA to a large pan of rapidly boiling water.
1 Cook pasta until just tender. Drain and return to pan. While pasta is cooking, allow spinach to thaw.
2 Melt butter in a heavy-based pan.

Add onion and garlic; cook over low heat, stirring regularly, for 5 minutes or until golden.
3 Add drained spinach, nutmeg, cream and stock to pan. Bring to boil and simmer for 3 minutes. Add salt and pepper. Add sauce to pasta and toss to combine. Serve in warmed pasta bowls. Sprinkle with pecorino cheese and serve immediately.

COOK'S FILE

Note: You can use fresh spinach—chop leaves; steam and add to sauce.

TORTELLINI WITH MUSHROOM SAUCE

Preparation time: 25 minutes
Total cooking time: 1 hour 30 minutes
Serves 4

Pasta
2 cups all-purpose flour
pinch salt
3 eggs
1 tablespoon olive oil
1 tablespoon water
water, extra

Filling
$\frac{1}{2}$ of a 9 oz package frozen
    spinach, thawed, excess
    liquid removed
4 oz ricotta cheese
2 tablespoons freshly grated
    Parmesan cheese
1 egg, beaten
salt and freshly ground black
    pepper to taste

Sauce
1 tablespoon olive oil
1 clove garlic, crushed
4 oz mushrooms, sliced
1 cup heavy cream
$\frac{1}{4}$ cup freshly grated Parmesan
    cheese
salt to taste
freshly ground black pepper
    to taste

➤ **TO MAKE PASTA:** Sift flour
and salt onto a board. Make a well in
the center of the flour.
1 In a jug, whisk together eggs, oil
and water. Add egg mixture gradually
to flour, working in with your hands
until mixture forms a ball. Add extra
water if necessary. Knead on a lightly
floured surface for 5 minutes or until
dough is smooth and elastic. Place the

dough in a lightly oiled bowl. Cover
with plastic wrap and allow to stand
for 30 minutes.
2 To make Filling: In a bowl, combine drained spinach, ricotta and
Parmesan cheeses, egg, salt and
pepper. Set aside.
3 To make Sauce: Heat oil in a frying pan. Add garlic and stir over low
heat for 30 seconds. Add mushrooms
and cook for 3 minutes. Pour in cream.
Set aside.
4 Roll dough out on a lightly floured
surface until about $\frac{1}{16}$ inch thick.
Using a floured cutter, cut into 2 inch
rounds. Spoon about $\frac{1}{2}$ teaspoon of
Filling in the center of each round.
Brush a little water around edge of
each round. Fold rounds in half to
form a semi-circle. Press edges together
firmly. Wrap each semi-circle around
your forefinger to form a ring. Press
ends of dough together firmly.
5 Cook tortellini in batches in a large
pan of rapidly boiling water for about
8 minutes each batch—until just
tender. Drain well and return to pan.
Keep warm.
6 Return Sauce to medium heat.
Bring to boil. Reduce heat and simmer
for 3 minutes. Add the Parmesan
cheese, salt and pepper; stir well. Add
Sauce to tortellini and toss until well
combined. Divide the tortellini and
sauce between individual warmed
serving bowls.

COOK'S FILE

Hints: Serve sprinkled with some
freshly grated Parmesan cheese and
chopped fresh parsley.

Steamed vegetables such as sliced
carrots, summer squash and zucchini
can be served separately. Alternatively,
serve with your choice of salad.
Note: Freshly made tortellini and
ravioli pastas are worth the extra care
and time—the results are delicious.

1

2

3

4

5

6

MACARONI CHEESE

Preparation time: 15 minutes
Total cooking time: 35 minutes
Serves 4

2 cups milk
1 cup heavy cream
1 bay leaf
1 whole clove
1/2 cinnamon stick
1/4 cup butter or margarine
2 tablespoons all-purpose flour
2 cups freshly grated cheddar
    cheese
1/2 cup freshly grated Parmesan
salt and freshly ground black
    pepper to taste

12 oz elbow macaroni
1 cup fresh bread crumbs
2 slices rindless bacon,
    chopped and fried
    until crisp

➤ PREHEAT OVEN to moderate
350°F.
1 Place milk and cream in a medium
pan with bay leaf, clove and cinnamon stick. Bring to boil. Remove from
heat. Allow to stand for 10 minutes.
Strain into a jug; remove and discard
flavorings.
2 Melt the butter in a medium pan.
Add the flour; stir over low heat 1
minute. Remove from heat. Gradually
add the milk and cream mixture, stirring until smooth. Return to heat.

Cook, stirring constantly, until sauce
boils and thickens. Reduce heat; simmer 3 minutes. Remove from the heat
and add 1 cup of cheddar cheese, 1/4
cup of Parmesan and salt and pepper.
Set aside.
3 Add macaroni to a large pan of
rapidly boiling water and cook until
just tender. Drain well and return to
pan. Add sauce and mix well. Spoon
into a deep casserole dish. Sprinkle
with combined bread crumbs, bacon
and remaining cheeses. Bake for
15–20 minutes or until golden. Serve.

C O O K ' S   F I L E

Variation: You can add chopped
cooked chicken to the white sauce
before mixing with the pasta.

PASTITSIO

Preparation time: 40 minutes
Total cooking time: 1 hour
Serves 4–6

8 oz tubular spaghetti
8 oz ricotta cheese
2 oz prosciutto, chopped
1 egg, beaten
1 tablespoon freshly grated
   Parmesan cheese
$1/4$ teaspoon ground nutmeg
salt and freshly ground black
   pepper to taste

Meat Sauce
2 tablespoons olive oil
1 onion, chopped
1 clove garlic, crushed
1 lb ground beef
16 oz can crushed tomatoes
$1/2$ cup red wine
$1/2$ cup beef stock
2 tablespoons tomato
   paste
2 tablespoons chopped fresh
   parsley
$1/2$ teaspoon ground oregano
salt and freshly ground black
   pepper to taste

Cheese Sauce
$1/4$ cup butter or margarine
$1/4$ cup all-purpose flour
$1^{1}/2$ cups milk
1 cup heavy cream
2 eggs, beaten
1 cup freshly grated cheddar
   cheese
$1/4$ teaspoon ground nutmeg
salt to taste
freshly ground black pepper to
   taste
$1/4$ cup fresh bread crumbs
$1/4$ cup freshly grated Parmesan
   cheese

➤ COOK PASTA in a large pan of boiling water until tender; drain, cool slightly and return to pan.

1   Oil an 11 x 8 inch ovenproof dish. Add ricotta, prosciutto, egg, Parmesan, nutmeg, salt and pepper to the cooked pasta. Press into dish. Set aside.

2 To make Meat Sauce: Heat oil in large pan. Add onion and garlic; stir over low heat until onion is tender. Add meat; brown well, breaking up with a fork as it cooks. Drain. Add undrained, crushed tomatoes, wine, stock, tomato paste, parsley, oregano, salt and pepper; stir. Bring to boil. Reduce heat. Simmer, uncovered, for 20 minutes. Spoon over the pasta layer. Set aside. Preheat oven to 350°F.

3 To make Cheese Sauce: Melt butter in medium pan. Add flour and cook, stirring, for 1 minute. Remove from heat. Gradually add milk and cream, stir until smooth. Return to heat. Cook, stirring constantly, until sauce boils and thickens. Reduce heat; simmer 3 minutes. Remove from heat. Whisk in eggs, cheese, nutmeg, salt and pepper. Spoon over meat layer. Sprinkle with combined bread crumbs and Parmesan. Bake 20–25 minutes.

COOK'S FILE

Storage time: Meat sauce can be made a day ahead and refrigerated.

RAVIOLI

Preparation time: 45 minutes +
   30 minutes standing
Total cooking time: 2 hours 45 minutes
Serves 4

Pasta
2 cups all-purpose flour
pinch salt
3 eggs
1 tablespoon olive oil
1 tablespoon water
1 egg yolk, extra
$1/4$ cup water, extra

Filling
4 oz ground chicken
$2^1/2$ oz ricotta or cottage cheese
2 oz chicken livers, trimmed
   and chopped
1 oz prosciutto, chopped
1 slice salami, chopped
2 tablespoons freshly grated
   Parmesan cheese
1 egg, beaten
1 tablespoon chopped fresh
   parsley
1 clove garlic, crushed
$1/4$ teaspoon pumpkin pie spice
salt and freshly ground black
   pepper to taste

Tomato Sauce
2 tablespoons olive oil
1 onion, finely chopped
2 cloves garlic, crushed
2 x 16 oz cans crushed tomatoes
$1/4$ cup chopped fresh basil
$1/2$ teaspoon mixed herbs
salt and freshly ground black
   pepper to taste

➤ **TO MAKE PASTA:** Sift flour
and salt onto a board. Make a well in
the center of the flour.

1 In a bowl, whisk together eggs, oil
and water. Add egg mixture gradually
to flour, working in with hand until
mixture forms a ball. Knead on a
lightly floured surface for 5 minutes
or until smooth and elastic. Place
dough in a lightly oiled bowl. Cover
with plastic wrap. Allow to stand for
30 minutes.

2 To make Filling: Place all ingredients in a food processor. Process
until finely chopped. Set aside.

3 To make Tomato Sauce: Heat
oil in a medium pan. Add onion and
garlic and stir over low heat until
onion is tender. Increase heat, add
undrained, crushed tomatoes, basil,
herbs, salt and pepper; stir. Bring to
boil. Reduce heat and simmer for 15
minutes. Remove from heat.

4 Roll out half the pasta dough until
$1/16$ inch thick. Cut with a knife or fluted pastry cutter into 4 inch strips.
Place teaspoons of filling at 2 inch
intervals down one side of each strip.
Whisk together extra egg yolk and
water. Brush along one side of dough
and between filling. Fold dough over
filling to meet the other side. Repeat
with remaining filling and dough.

5 Press the edges of dough together
firmly to seal. Cut between the
mounds of filling with a knife or a
fluted pastry cutter.

6 Cook ravioli in batches in a large
pan of rapidly boiling water for
10 minutes each batch. Reheat
Tomato Sauce in a large pan. Add
cooked ravioli and toss well until
sauce is evenly distributed. Simmer,
stirring, for 5 minutes. Garnish with
sprigs of fresh herbs, if desired.

COOK'S FILE

Hint: Serve with crusty bread and a
light salad.
Note: If preferred, pasta dough may
be made with only 2 eggs— however, it
will require extra kneading.

4

5

6

BAKED CANNELLONI MILANESE

Preparation time: 20 minutes
Total cooking time: 1 hour 50 minutes
Serves 4

1 lb ground pork and veal
1/2 cup dry bread crumbs
1/2 cup freshly grated Parmesan
    cheese
2 eggs, beaten
1 teaspoon dried oregano
salt and freshly ground black
    pepper to taste
12–15 cannelloni tubes
12 oz fresh ricotta cheese
1/2 cup freshly grated Parmesan
    cheese
1/2 cup freshly grated cheddar
    cheese

Tomato Sauce
13 1/2 fl oz can tomato puree
13 1/2 oz can crushed tomatoes
2 cloves garlic, crushed
1/4 cup chopped fresh basil
freshly ground black pepper
    to taste

➤ PREHEAT OVEN to moderate 350°F. Lightly grease a rectangular casserole dish.

1 In a medium bowl, combine meat, bread crumbs, Parmesan cheese, beaten egg, oregano and seasonings. Use a teaspoon to stuff the cannelloni tubes with meat mixture. Set aside.

2 To make Tomato Sauce: Place tomato puree, undrained, crushed tomatoes and garlic in medium pan. Bring to boil. Reduce heat. Simmer for 15 minutes. Add basil and pepper and stir well.

3 Spoon half the Tomato Sauce over the base of prepared dish.

4 Arrange the stuffed cannelloni tubes on top. Cover with remaining sauce. Spread with ricotta cheese. Sprinkle with combined Parmesan and cheddar cheeses. Bake, covered with foil, for 1 hour. Uncover and bake for another 15 minutes or until golden. Cut into squares for serving.

COOK'S FILE

Hint: Serve with tomato quarters and mixed green salad. Garnish with sprigs of fresh herbs.

1

2

3

4

BAKED FETTUCCINE

Preparation time: 20 minutes
Total cooking time: 25 minutes
Serves 4

1 lb spinach fettuccine
$^{1}/_{4}$ cup butter or margarine
1 onion, finely chopped
8 fl oz carton sour cream
1 cup heavy cream
$^{1}/_{4}$ teaspoon ground nutmeg
$^{1}/_{2}$ cup freshly grated Parmesan

salt to taste
freshly ground black pepper to taste
1 cup freshly grated mozzarella cheese

➤ PREHEAT OVEN to moderate 350°F.

1 Add fettuccine to a large pan of rapidly boiling water and cook until just tender. Drain well and set aside. While pasta is cooking, melt butter in a large pan. Add onion and stir over low heat until onion is tender. Add fettuccine to pan.

2 Add sour cream to pan and toss well. Simmer, stirring, until pasta is well coated.

3 Add cream, nutmeg, $^{1}/_{4}$ cup Parmesan, salt and pepper; stir. Pour into a greased casserole dish. Sprinkle with the combined mozzarella and remaining Parmesan. Bake for 15 minutes or until the cheese is softened and golden.

COOK'S FILE

Note: Do not use fat-free cream.

CLASSIC LASAGNA

Preparation time: 25 minutes
Total cooking time: 1 hour 15 minutes
Serves 4–6

8 oz package no-cook lasagna
   sheets
1/2 cup freshly grated mozzarella
   cheese
1/2 cup freshly grated cheddar
   cheese
1/2 cup heavy cream
1/4 cup freshly grated Parmesan
   cheese

Cheese Sauce
1/4 cup butter or margarine
1/3 cup all-purpose flour
2 cups milk
1 cup freshly grated cheddar
   cheese
salt and pepper to taste

Meat Sauce
1 tablespoon olive oil
1 onion, finely chopped
1 clove garlic, crushed
1 lb ground beef
2 x 16 oz cans crushed tomatoes
1/4 cup red wine
1/2 teaspoon ground oregano
1/4 teaspoon ground basil
salt and freshly ground black
   pepper to taste

➤ PREHEAT OVEN to moderate 350°F.

1 Brush a shallow oblong ovenproof dish (approximately 9 x 13 inch) with melted butter or oil. Line with lasagna sheets, breaking them to fill any gaps. Set aside.

2 To make Cheese Sauce: Melt butter in a medium pan. Add flour and stir for 1 minute. Remove from heat. Gradually add milk, stirring until mixture is smooth. Return to heat. Cook, stirring constantly, over medium heat until sauce boils and thickens. Reduce heat, simmer for 3 minutes. Remove from heat, add cheese, salt and pepper; stir until well combined. Set aside.

3 To make Meat Sauce: Heat the olive oil in a large pan. Add onion and garlic and stir over low heat until onion is tender. Add ground beef. Brown well, breaking up any lumps

with a fork as it cooks. Drain. Stir in the undrained, crushed tomatoes, wine, oregano, basil, salt and pepper. Bring to boil. Reduce the heat; simmer for 20 minutes.

4 Spoon one-third of the meat sauce over the lasagna sheets. Top with one-third of the cheese sauce. Arrange a layer of lasagna sheets over top.

5 Continue layering, finishing with lasagna sheets. Sprinkle with the combined mozzarella and cheddar cheese.

6 Pour cream over the top. Sprinkle with Parmesan. Bake for 35–40 minutes or until bubbling and golden.

COOK'S FILE

Note: Cheese sauce is a variation of Béchamel Sauce. A true Béchamel uses milk infused with flavorings such as bay leaf, cloves, peppercorns, parsley sprig and cinnamon stick. To do this, bring milk to boiling point (without boiling—known as scalding) with one or more of the flavorings and allow to stand for 10 minutes before straining. To prevent sauce forming a skin, cover surface completely with plastic wrap or greased wax paper until required.

Sauces are easier to handle if allowed to cool before layering.

PASTA AND SPINACH TIMBALE

Preparation time: 15 minutes
Total cooking time: 35 minutes
Serves 6

2 tablespoons butter
1 tablespoon olive oil
1 onion, chopped
1 bunch cooked, drained spinach
8 eggs, beaten
1 cup heavy cream
4 oz spaghetti or tagliolini, cooked
1/2 cup freshly grated cheddar cheese

1/2 cup freshly grated Parmesan cheese
salt and freshly ground black pepper to taste

➤ PREHEAT OVEN to moderate 350°F. Brush six 1-cup capacity molds with melted butter or oil. Line bases with parchment paper.

1 Heat butter and oil together in a frying pan. Add onion and stir over low heat until onion is tender. Add well-drained spinach and cook for 1 minute. Remove from heat and allow to cool. Whisk in eggs and cream. Stir in the spaghetti or tagliolini, grated cheeses, salt and pepper; stir well. Spoon into prepared molds.

2 Place the molds in a baking dish. Pour boiling water into baking dish to come halfway up sides of molds. Bake for 30–35 minutes or until set. Halfway through cooking, you may need to cover the top with a sheet of foil to prevent excess browning. Near the end of the cooking time, test the timbales with the point of a knife. When they are cooked, the knife should come out clean.

3 Allow the timbales to rest for 15 minutes. Run point of a knife around edge of each mold. Invert onto serving plates.

COOK'S FILE

Hints: Serve with a tomato sauce.

PASTA PIE

Preparation time: 15 minutes
Total cooking time: 55 minutes
Serves 4

8 oz macaroni
1 tablespoon olive oil
1 onion, sliced
4 oz pancetta, chopped
4 oz ham, chopped
4 eggs
1 cup milk
1 cup heavy cream
2 tablespoons snipped chives

salt to taste
freshly ground black pepper to
  taste
1 cup freshly grated cheddar
  cheese
4 oz bocconcini (approximately
  4), chopped

➤ PREHEAT OVEN to moderate 350°F.

1 Add the macaroni to a large pan of rapidly boiling water and cook until just tender. Drain thoroughly. Spread evenly over the base of a 2 inch deep casserole dish.

2 Heat oil in a large pan. Add sliced onion and stir over low heat until the onion is tender. Add the chopped pancetta to the pan and cook for 2 minutes. Add the ham to the mixture and stir well. Remove from heat; allow to cool.

3 In a bowl, whisk together eggs, milk, cream, chives, salt and pepper. Add cheddar cheese, chopped bocconcini and the pancetta mixture; stir well. Spread evenly over the top of macaroni. Bake for 35–40 minutes or until mixture is set.

COOK'S FILE

Hint: Serve with slices of roma tomato.

TORTELLINI WITH MUSHROOM AND GRUYERE SAUCE

Preparation time: 15 minutes
Total cooking time: 25 minutes
Serves 4–6

1 lb fresh or dried chicken- or
   veal-filled herb tortellini
1/3 cup butter
3 scallions, chopped
6 1/2 oz baby mushrooms, sliced
2 tablespoons all-purpose flour

1 1/2 cups milk
1/2 cup heavy cream
3 1/3 oz freshly grated gruyère
   cheese
salt and freshly ground black
   pepper to taste
1/2 cup pine nuts, toasted

➤ BRING A LARGE PAN of water to
the boil.
1 Add tortellini and cook until just
tender. Drain and keep warm.
2 Melt half the butter in a medium
pan, add scallions and sliced mushrooms. Cook over medium heat for

3 minutes or until softened. Set aside.
3 In another pan, melt remaining
butter. Add flour and stir over low
heat for 2 minutes. Gradually add
milk and cream, stirring constantly
until sauce boils and thickens. Add
cheese and season to taste; stir well.
Combine with mushrooms. Arrange
tortellini in a serving bowl; pour sauce
over and sprinkle with pine nuts and
extra chopped scallions, if desired.

COOK'S FILE

Note: Gruyère is a hard full-flavored
cheese that melts easily.

PASTA-FILLED VEGETABLES

Preparation time: 20 minutes
Total cooking time: 45 minutes
Serves 4–6

1 tablespoon olive oil
1 onion, finely chopped
1 clove garlic, crushed
3 slices Canadian bacon, finely
    chopped
5 oz orzo, cooked
1 cup freshly grated mozzarella
    cheese
1/2 cup freshly grated Parmesan
    cheese
2 tablespoons chopped fresh
    parsley
4 large red peppers, halved
    lengthwise, seeds removed
16 oz can crushed tomatoes
1/2 cup dry white wine
1 tablespoon tomato paste
1/2 teaspoon ground oregano
salt and freshly ground black
    pepper to taste
2 tablespoons chopped fresh basil

➤ PREHEAT OVEN to moderate
350°F. Lightly oil a large shallow
ovenproof dish.

1 Heat oil in a pan. Add onion and
garlic and stir over low heat until onion
is tender. Add bacon; stir until crisp.

2 Transfer bacon mixture to large
bowl and combine with orzo, cheeses
and parsley. Spoon mixture into pepper
halves. Arrange in dish.

3 In a bowl, combine undrained,
crushed tomatoes, wine, tomato paste,
oregano, salt and pepper. Spoon over
orzo mixture. Sprinkle with basil.
Bake for 35–40 minutes.

COOK'S FILE

Hint: Serve with baked chicken.

PASTA SOUFFLE

Preparation time: 20 minutes
Total cooking time: 55 minutes
Serves 4

2 tablespoons freshly grated
   Parmesan cheese
1/4 cup butter or margarine
1 small onion, finely chopped
2 tablespoons all-purpose flour
2 cups milk
1/2 cup chicken stock
3 eggs, separated
4 oz small macaroni, cooked
6 3/4 oz can salmon, drained and
   flaked
1 tablespoon chopped fresh
   parsley
grated rind of 1 lemon
salt and freshly ground black
   pepper to taste

➤ PREHEAT OVEN to hot 425°F.
1 Brush a round 7 inch (6-cup capacity) soufflé dish with oil. Coat base and sides with Parmesan. Shake off excess.
To Collar a Soufflé Dish: Cut a piece of aluminium foil or wax paper 2 inches longer than the circumference of a round 7 inch (6-cup capacity) soufflé dish. Fold foil in half lengthwise. Wrap foil around the outside of the soufflé dish; it should extend 2 inches above the rim. Secure foil with string.
2 Heat butter in a large pan. Add onion and cook over low heat until tender. Add flour. Stir 2 minutes or until mixture is lightly golden. Remove from heat. Gradually blend in milk and stock, stirring until mixture is smooth. Return to heat. Stir constantly over medium heat until mixture boils and thickens. Reduce heat and simmer for 3 minutes. Add egg yolks and whisk until smooth. Add

macaroni, salmon, parsley, lemon rind, salt and pepper. Stir until combined. Transfer mixture to a large bowl.
3 Using electric beaters, beat egg whites in a small dry mixing bowl until stiff peaks form. Using a metal spoon, fold gently into salmon mixture. Spoon into prepared dish. Bake for 40–45 minutes or until well risen and browned. Serve immediately.

COOK'S FILE

Storage time: Hot soufflés should be made just before you want to serve them as they will collapse very quickly after removal from the oven. The base mixture can be prepared, up to the end of Step 2, well in advance. Soften the mixture before folding in beaten egg whites. Whites should be folded into mixture just before cooking.

1

2

3

BAKED MEATBALLS AND PASTA

Preparation time: 25 minutes
Total cooking time: 55 minutes
Serves 4

4 oz macaroni
1 lb ground beef
1 onion, finely chopped
$^{1}/_{2}$ cup fresh bread crumbs
2 tablespoons freshly grated
   Parmesan cheese
1 tablespoon chopped fresh basil
1 egg, beaten
2 tablespoons olive oil
1 cup freshly grated mozzarella
   cheese
$^{1}/_{2}$ cup fresh bread crumbs

Sauce
1 onion, sliced
1 clove garlic, crushed
1 green pepper, seeded and sliced
4 oz mushrooms, sliced
$^{1}/_{4}$ cup tomato paste
1 cup water
$^{1}/_{2}$ cup red wine
salt and freshly ground black
   pepper to taste

➤ ADD MACARONI TO a large pan
of rapidly boiling water and cook
until just tender. Drain, set aside.
1 In a bowl, combine ground beef,
onion, bread crumbs, Parmesan, basil
and egg. Form heaped teaspoonfuls
into small balls.
2 Heat oil in a frying pan. Add meatballs and cook until well browned.
Drain on paper towels. Transfer to
an ovenproof dish. Preheat oven to
moderate 350°F.
3 To make Sauce: Add onion and
garlic to same pan; stir over low heat
until onion is tender. Add pepper and
mushrooms; cook 2 minutes. Stir in
tomato paste. Add combined water
and wine to pan. Bring to boil, stirring. Mix in macaroni, salt and
pepper. Pour over top of meatballs.
4 Bake, uncovered, for 30–35 minutes. Sprinkle with combined mozzarella cheese and bread crumbs. Bake
for another 10 minutes or until golden.

COOK'S FILE

Note: Macaroni comes in many
different shapes and sizes—choose
whichever you prefer.

SEMOLINA GNOCCHI

Preparation time: 15 minutes +
 1 hour refrigeration
Total cooking time: 40 minutes
Serves 4

3 cups milk
¼ teaspoon ground nutmeg
salt and freshly ground black
 pepper to taste
²/₃ cup semolina
1 egg, beaten
1½ cups freshly grated
 Parmesan cheese

¼ cup butter, melted
½ cup heavy cream
½ cup freshly grated mozzarella
 cheese
¼ teaspoon ground nutmeg,
 extra

➤ LINE A DEEP 11 x 7 x 1½ inch
baking pan with parchment paper.
1 Place milk, nutmeg, salt and pepper
in a medium pan. Bring to boil.
Reduce heat and gradually stir in
semolina. Cook, stirring occasionally,
for 5–10 minutes or until semolina is
very stiff. Remove from heat. Add egg
and 1 cup Parmesan cheese to semolina

mixture; stir to combine. Spread mixture in prepared pan. Refrigerate for 1
hour or until firm.
2 Preheat oven to moderate 350°F.
Cut semolina into rounds using a
floured 1½ inch cutter. Arrange in a
greased shallow casserole dish.
3 Pour butter over the top, followed
by the cream. Sprinkle with the combined remaining Parmesan and mozzarella cheese. Sprinkle with extra
nutmeg. Bake for 20–25 minutes or
until golden.

COOK'S FILE

Hint: Serve with mixed salad.

INDEX

USEFUL INFORMATION

All the recipes in this book have been double-tested by our team of home economists to ensure high standards of accuracy. All the cup and spoon measurements used are level. We have used large (2 oz) eggs in all of the recipes. The sizes of cans available vary from manufacturer to manufacturer and between countries—use the can size closest to the one suggested in the recipe.

Glossary of Terms

Al dente: Italian cookery term for cooking pasta eg: spaghetti, until just tender.

Blanch: To plunge vegetables into boiling water for about 1 minute, then plunge into ice cold water. This helps them retain their color, crispness and nutritional value.

Cracked pepper: Small pieces of cracked peppercorns made in a coarse grinder. May be bought ready ground.

Devein shrimp: A process to remove the digestive tract by using tweezers or a slight incision down the back after the shell is removed.

Garnish: An edible trimming on the dish to add color and enhance appearance.

Peeling tomatoes: To remove the skin from a tomato: mark a small cross on the bottom, then plunge the tomato into boiling water for 1–2 minutes. Then plunge into cold water. Peel skin down from the cross.

Process: To use either a food processor or a blender to finely chop or puree ingredients.

Shred: To slice or shave in a downward motion using a large chef's knife. On firm vegetables such as carrots, use a scraper for shredding.

Simmer: To heat a liquid until small bubbles form and it is on the point of boiling.

Oven Temperatures

Cooking times may vary slightly depending on the type of oven you are using. Before you preheat the oven, we suggest that you refer to the manufacturer's instructions to ensure proper temperature control.

For convection ovens check your appliance manual, but as a general rule, you will need to set the oven temperature a little lower than the temperature indicated in the recipe.

	°F
Very slow	250
Slow	300
Warm	325
Moderate	350
Mod. hot	375
Mod. hot	400
Hot	425
Very hot	450

Cup Conversions

1 cup bread crumbs,	dry	= 3 $1/3$ oz
	fresh	= 2 $2/3$ oz
1 cup cheese, grated		
	cheddar (firmly packed)	= 4 oz
	mozzarella	= 4 $3/4$ oz
	Parmesan	= 3 $1/3$ oz
1 cup all-purpose flour		= 4 oz
	wholewheat	= 4 $3/4$ oz
1 cup pasta, short (eg. macaroni)		= 5 oz
1 cup semolina		= 4 oz

Copyright© Text, design, photography and illustrations Murdoch Books® 1995.
All rights reserved under International and Pan-American Copyright Conventions.

No part of this book may be reproduced or transmitted in any form or by any means electronic or mechanical including photocopying, recording, or by any information storage and retrieval system, without permission in writing from the publisher.

This 1997 Crescent edition is published by Random House Value Publishing, Inc.,
201 East 50th Street, New York, N.Y. 10022.

Random House
New York·Toronto·London·Sydney·Auckland
http://www.randomhouse.com/

Printed and bound in the United States of America.

A CIP catalog record for this book is available from the Library of Congress
ISBN 0-517-18395-1

8 7 6 5 4 3 2 1